Volume 19, Number 2　　　　　　　　　　　　　**2004**

Contents

Subscriber Information

Journal of Mass Media Ethics (ISSN 0890–0523) is published quarterly by Lawrence Erlbaum Associates, Inc., 10 Industrial Avenue, Mahwah, NJ 07430–2262. Subscriptions for Volume 19, 2004, are available only on a calendar-year basis.

Individual rates: **Print *Plus* Online:** $40.00 in US/Canada, $70.00 outside US/Canada. Institutional rates: **Print-Only:** $340.00 in US/Canada, $370.00 outside US/Canada. **Online-Only:** $320.00 in US/Canada and outside US/Canada. **Print *Plus* Online:** $375.00 in US/Canada, $405.00 outside US/Canada. Visit LEA's Web site at http://www.erlbaum.com to view free sample.

Order subscriptions through the Journal Subscription Department, Lawrence Erlbaum Associates, Inc., 10 Industrial Avenue, Mahwah, NJ 07430–2262.

Change of Address: Send change-of-address notice to Journal Subscription Department, Lawrence Erlbaum Associates, Inc., 10 Industrial Avenue, Mahwah, NJ 07430–2262.

Claims for missing issues cannot be honored beyond 4 months after mailing date. Duplicate copies cannot be sent to replace issues not delivered due to failure to notify publisher of change of address.

Journal of Mass Media Ethics is abstracted or indexed in *Communication Abstracts; Communication Institute for Online Scholarships; Columbia Journalism Review; ComIndex; Media and Values; Nordicom Finland; Public Affairs Information Service; Com Abstracts; Humanities Index; Humanities Abstracts;* EBSCO*host* Products.

Microform copies of this journal are available through ProQuest Information and Learning, P.O. Box 1346, Ann Arbor, MI 48106–1346. For more information, call 1–800–521–0600, ext. 2888.

Requests for permission should be sent to the Permissions Department, Lawrence Erlbaum Associates, Inc., 10 Industrial Avenue, Mahwah, NJ 07430–2262.

Journal of Mass Media Ethics, *19*(2), 81–85
Copyright © 2004, Lawrence Erlbaum Associates, Inc.

Foreword

This issue comprises a selection of papers presented at the Inaugural International Media Ethics Conference held in Canberra, Australia from July 3rd to 4th, 2002. The conference, "Ethics, Media Credibility, and Global Standards," was hosted by the Centre for Applied Philosophy and Public Ethics (CAPPE); John Fairfax Holdings and News Limited in association with the Key Centre for Ethics, Law, Justice and Governance (Griffith University, Queensland, Australia); and the St. James Ethics Centre (Sydney, Australia). CAPPE is an Australian Research Council funded Special Research Centre attached to Charles Sturt University, the University of Melbourne, and the Australian National University.

The primary aim of the conference was to bring together media professionals from leading journalism, advertising, and public relations organizations and institutions and media regulating bodies with academics from within and outside Australia for the purpose of engaging in dialogue concerning ethical issues that impact on professional standards and practice in relation to professional credibility and public trust; specifically, the bond of trust that governs the media's relationship with the public and government.

Leading keynote speakers included Geoffrey Nyarota, Editor in Chief of *Daily News*, Zimbabwe; Fred Hilmer, Fairfax Chief Executive Officer; Michael Stutchbury, Editor of *The Australian*; Jack Waterford, Editor of the *Canberra Times*; David Flint, Chairman of the Australian Broadcasting Authority; Charles Sampford, Director, Key Centre Law, Justice and Governance; and from the United States, Jay Black, then Poynter–Jamison Chair in Media Ethics, University of South Florida (USF) St. Petersburg and Editor of the *Journal of Mass Media Ethics* (*JMME*); Deni Elliott, then Director of Practical Ethics Center, University of Montana (Black has since retired from the Poynter–Jamison Chair, and Elliott has moved into that position at USF St. Petersburg); and Tom Brislin, University of Hawaii. The articles selected for this issue are representative of some of the central themes of the conference, such as

- Managing the newsroom and editorial independence.
- Limits on press freedom.
- Ethical standards and credibility.
- Investigative journalism.
- Commercial constraints on the media.

A common theme that emerged from a number of articles at the conference was a need for an integrated ethical, legal, and regulated approach to media ethics that takes into account not only the actions of individual media practitioners but equally those of the organizations in which they are placed as well as the actions, codes, regulations, and policies of the whole media industry to which those organizations belong. Ethics, it seems, in the media as well as in all other professions and institutions, requires a division of ethical labor, one shared by individual practitioners, organizations, industry institutions, regulatory bodies, and last but not least, governments.

Sampford and Lui, in their article, argue for a media ethics regime that employs an ethical risk management approach to media ethics not unlike that employed routinely in assessing financial risk and strategies for minimizing that risk in business and other institutional corporations. The ethics regime Sampford and Lui propose

> Takes a coordinated, comprehensive, and holistic approach that involves the formulation and implementation of regulatory ideals and mechanisms at multiple levels and domains of activities—from voluntary forms of self-regulation such as ethics codes to more interventionist strategies such as government regulations.

The primary aim of this holistic and integrated strategy is the development of a systematic regulatory framework or a media integrity regime for the minimization if not elimination of the ethical risk that is inherent in media organizations, the risk that emanates as a result of the potentially conflicting functions of being both reliable and trustworthy providers of information to the public as well as businesses whose operative aim in a market environment is to make a profit. Such a risk, if not anticipated and appropriately controlled, can generate conflicts of interest that undermine the integrity and credibility of those two separate but interrelated functions.

Although recognizing, along with a number of other speakers at the conference, the vital importance of ethical standards that "emphasize character and rely on modifying the conduct of individuals" Sampford and Lui argue that such ethical standards, although necessary, are insufficient for establishing effective ethics in the media. What is required, Sampford and Lui argue, is "an ethics regime that includes a set of ethical standards but also includes a number of legal and institutional means to realize those standards."

The insufficiency of moral character for establishing ethics in any profession, industry, or institution, including the media, is a central theme emphasized also by Neil Levy. By drawing on experiments conducted by social psychologist Stanley Milgram, Levy is able to argue that character, although necessary for moral conduct, is perhaps not always sufficient. In certain situations, specific circumstances may conspire to undermine and compromise the moral intentions of an agent who would normally, but not in the situations in question, act out of moral character. Levy goes on to claim that "the situational pressures that characterize journalism, at least as it is structured today, are therefore likely to overwhelm the resources of character, no matter how good our education, no matter how virtuous our students." In consonance with Sampford and Lui, Levy proposes that although a good character is relevant to journalism, the formation of character nevertheless is "a process that requires a conducive environment, which is to say an environment shaped by regulations." What Levy perhaps has in mind is an integrated ethics regime similar to the one advocated by Sampford and Lui.

In his article, Ian Richards, like Sampford and Lui, also reflects on the inherent conflict between the media's function as providers of information to the public and their function as corporate businesses whose primary aim is to make money for their shareholders. To emphasize this inherent conflict, Richards refers to "Milton Friedman's much-quoted statement that 'the business of business is business' (Friedman, 1970, p. 124)."

According to Richards, what underlies this ethically problematic conflict and helps provide a possible but not surefire answer to its solution is the contrast between shareholders and "stakeholders." According to Richards, the notion of stakeholders is useful in journalism because it enables us to see that in media organizations like in other organizations, there are a number of different stakeholders whose ethical interests may be as equally legitimate and worthy of consideration as those of corporate shareholders. Richards, however, raises a skeptical, and in my opinion valid, challenge to the view just canvassed: How can the conflicting interests of all these different stakeholders be balanced? One attempt to answer this challenge to which Richards refers is the social responsibility theory approach that "involves an acceptance of 'a commitment to the public good that outweighs short-term individual self-interests'(Day, 1997, p. 34)."

The problem, of course, with this approach at the theoretical level at which the solution is offered is the amoralist challenge: Why should the public good take precedence over self-interest? In the absence of a rationally compelling argument that demonstrates that the public good should always trump self-interest, the solution offered by the social responsibility theory lacks dialectical force even if it does sound nice. Although not directly discussed by Richards, the amoralist challenge is alluded to at the end of his article with an ethically poignant and important statement: "It is worth reminding ourselves that the underlying force that drives business ethics is the same basic question that underlies journalism ethics: Why be ethical?" Referred to in ethical theory as the authoritative question of morality, it is a question that should be given more serious attention by professional ethicists. As Plato pointed out in Book 2 of the *Republic,* it is the most fundamental and important question in ethics and not least in professional ethics, including media ethics.

Finally, in his article "Empowerment as a Universal Ethic in Global Journalism," Tom Brislin seems to give preference to the notion of autonomy over that of truth. Brislin refers to the latter as an admirable but very "spongy" imperative, "difficult to measure and subject to multiple claims and self-justifying interpretations. Autonomy, on the other hand, is equally admirable and somewhat easier to measure." The thrust of Brislin's argument is "that the autonomy of journalists is reflective of (although not necessarily proportional to) the autonomy of the citizenry in any given state. Autonomy empowers journalists to practice their professionalism, which in turn offers the potential to empower the citizenry." Brislin goes on to say that "journalists deal in truth as a raw material in the production of meaning through storytelling." My concern with this approach is that if we accept that truth is not necessary for empowerment and if "storytelling" by autonomous journalists can empower the citizenry through fiction rather than truth, would the citizenry be adequately informed to make choices that render their theoretical assumed autonomy meaningful and useful in practice? As demonstrated in Nazi Germany, storytelling in the form of political propaganda can be empowering without it being ethical or useful.

Taking a global perspective, Brislin argues that whereas

> Many Western European, Japanese, Taiwanese, and Korean news organizations are comfortable with an advocacy model, in effect "wearing their politics on their sleeves," achieving balance in aggregate, rather than within each organization. ... The mainstream U.S. press, bound in what some would call a cult of objectivity, is often criticized for emphasizing problems without solutions, treating politics as a spectator sport rather than a participant sport, and for treating its constituents as consumers.

Brislin concludes his article with a question and a challenge: "Is empowerment a reasonable measuring stick and standard for "the Restern world"—the multitude of non-Western systems that are fellow travelers on the superhighway of globalization?" As a possible answer or at least a source to an answer, Brislin proposes that

> Future studies of comparative press systems, practices, standards, and values should include a focus on the degree of autonomy the journalist enjoys within legal, cultural, and professional limits and how that autonomy is

translated into an ethic of empowerment that both reflects the changes of globalization and respects indigenous value systems.

Such a quest will, I believe, be greatly assisted by developing media values that are universal and transcend the political, cultural, and other local ethical idiosyncrasies of particular countries. Although I agree with Brislin that truth can be a spongy concept, it should nevertheless be the primary measuring standard for all journalists all over the world, for ultimately it is truth that empowers us by setting us free from prejudice, fear, and mistrust.

I would like to thank the *JMME* editors for the opportunity to coedit this collection of articles. I also thank the authors of these articles for their most kind cooperation in putting together this issue. Last but not least, I thank Aaron Quinn for his most diligent assistance in editing these articles.

Edward Spence
Centre for Applied Philosophy and Public Ethics
Charles Sturt University
New South Wales, Australia

Editors' note: This issue of *JMME* also includes a Cases and Commentaries section plus book reviews. The case study examines the perplexing problem of plagiarism, an issue brought to our attention by freelancer Sharon Schnall. Responding to her dilemma are veteran editor Tim McGuire, National Public Radio ombudsman Jeffrey Dvorkin, and media ethicist Sandra Borden. Books reviewed in this issue are on media effects research and Tom Wicker's insider's guide to journalism.

Journal of Mass Media Ethics, 19(2), 86–107

Australian Media Ethics Regime and Ethical Risk Management

Charles Sampford and Robyn Lui

Griffith University, Brisbane, Australia

❏ *Media organizations are simultaneously key elements of an effective democracy and, for the most part, commercial entities seeking success in the market. They play an essential role in the formation of public opinion and the influence on personal choices. Yet most of them are commercial enterprises seeking readers or viewers, advertising, favorable regulatory decisions for their media, and other assets. This creates some intrinsic difficulties and produces some sharp tensions within media ethics. In this article, we examine such tensions—in theory and practice. We then consider the feasibility of introducing an ethics regime to the media industry—a regime that would be effective in a deregulated environment in protecting public interest and social responsibility. In the article, we also outline a rationale and a methodology for the institutionalization of an acceptable and workable media ethics regime that aims to protect the integrity of the industry in a future of undoubtedly increasing commercial pressure.*

Market, Media, and Democracy

The idea that the media play a central role in the maintenance of democratic society has framed debates about media ethics. The implicit contract between the media and the functioning of democracy underpins the claims of journalists for a substantial degree of autonomy. The media provide a public service. They are considered the fourth estate. A healthy democracy requires, among other things, the participation of informed citizens, and one of the roles of the media, if not the most important one, is to enhance the level of participation by providing the information and analyses on a range of political, economic, and social issues. Belsey and Chadwick (1999) framed the issue in this way: "Given the importance of the media to society as a whole, how then can the social responsibility and integrity of the media be protected and promoted?" (p. 55).

This question is complicated by the fact that the crucial public role is largely played by private corporations. The media industry is increasingly difficult to regulate due not only to technological developments and globalization of media conglomerates but also the trend to contractual relationships between the suppliers of information and entertainment and their audience. However, despite these trends and despite the commercial interests of most media organizations, the media continue to play an ongoing critical role in the formation of public opinion. We argue that if the public interest is to be served, the integrity of the role should be recognized and enhanced rather than compromised. We start from the premise that to inform citizens and foster democratic dialogue are the primary functions of the media. These twin purposes underpin our current undertaking to develop a systematic regulatory framework or a media integrity regime.[1]

In this article, we address the public integrity and accountability of the media industry as a whole as it relates to the formation of and influence on public opinion. We consider the feasibility of introducing an ethics regime to the media industry—a regime that would be effective in a deregulated environment in protecting public interest and social responsibility. We also outline a rationale and a methodology for the institutionalization of an acceptable and workable media ethics regime that aims to protect the integrity of the industry in a future of undoubtedly increasing commercial pressure.[2]

Rationale for Establishing an Ethics Regime Within Australian Media

Recognizing the Intrinsic Difficulties of Media Ethics

In modern liberal democracies, the majority of citizens value both democracy and the market, and there is popular commitment to the belief that politics should be dominated by democratic principles, and the economy should be dominated by market principles. Although both democracy and the market are built on the single principle of individual choice, they involve two fundamentally different principles for evaluating choices. The principle for democracy is "one vote one value"; the principle for the market is "one dollar one value." The eternal temptation is for those who have accumulated dollars in the market to use those dollars to influence those decisions that are supposed to be governed by democratic principles. Accordingly, defining and policing the boundaries between the market and democracy is a perennial problem in modern liberal societies committed to both democratic and market principles. It gives rise to some of the most difficult and controversial issues in liberal democracies.

Media institutions face particular dilemmas because they are simultaneously key elements of an effective democracy and, for the most part, commercial entities seeking success in the market. They play an essential role in the formation of public opinion and the influence on personal choices. Yet most of them are commercial enterprises seeking not only readers, listeners, and viewers but also advertising revenue, favorable government decisions about media policy, and where they own nonmedia assets, favorable policies on those issues as well. There is an oft-stated concern that those commercial activities and interests in the market might distort the role that media institutions play in the formation of public opinion and consequentially in our democracy. There is the opposite concern that the privileged access that media corporations will gain from politicians seeking a good press may skew decisions politicians have to make in a way that distorts or even undermines markets.

> *Media institutions face particular*
> *dilemmas because they are*
> *simultaneously key elements of*
> *an effective democracy and, for*
> *the most part, commercial*
> *entities seeking success in the*
> *market.*

One of these problems is the widespread attempt to influence public debate through the buying of advertising space or, in the cash-for-comment scandal, in buying the commentary. Although quality newspapers try to erect a firewall between journalists and sellers of advertising space, in some sections and in many magazines, the firewall has many convenient access doors. In the recent cash-for-comment scandal, the doors were wide enough for those who were seeking to influence public opinion to bring through wheelbarrows of cash from those who were willing to pay for talk-back radio hosts to speak well of them.[3]

One of the starkest expressions of this potential problem comes from a story about Lord Beaverbrook. After the purchase of the *Telegraph* and *Evening Standard*, a puzzled interlocutor asked, given the apparently limited financial returns that could be expected, why Beaverbrook had bought it. Beaverbrook's answer was simple: "power." By this, Beaverbrook clearly meant political power. We do not believe this is a goal that can be justified in a democracy. It would allow the market to dominate our polity. The media do not then stand astride both camps but are the means by which one sphere dominates the other.

No media owner today would be as crass as to say as much in public. It may be that no media owner would even think it in private. However, the very perception of such a thought might influence the decisions of politicians. If they believe media corporations might use that power, politicians may avoid actions that might conflict with the interests of media corporations and their owners and may act in ways that they believe further the interests of those they would like to speak well of them at election time.

What is more, some are tempted to think that there is nothing wrong with this activity. "It's his newspaper: It's his money." A former chairman of the board of a major media group first related the Beaverbrook story to Sampford not as a criticism of Beaverbrook but as a part of the natural order of things. The comment stimulated our thinking on the way that the media straddle the democracy–market interface. It prompted us to reflect on the importance of professional journalism in maintaining that divide. This is not to say that the professional ethics of journalists can be effective by itself but that it is a key part of the equation—whereas the political and economic preferences of the owner are not.

We draw an analogy—in the relationship between medical professionals and their employers. Private hospital ownership does not override the professional duties of the medical staff. It would be unthinkable for the owner of a hospital to interfere with the diagnosis of patients under his or her employee's care. However, it is not just a matter of leaving it all in the hands of the individual doctor. The individual doctor cannot expend unlimited hospital resources, and the hospital has to decide the kind of services it offers. Similarly, the journalist cannot unilaterally decide what to write, how long it will be, and where it will be placed. Such decisions have to be taken institutionally and involve a number of different professionals.

This is not, in fact, a problem confined to doctors and journalists. It involves any professional employed by an organization—including corporate lawyers and accountants as well as internal auditors. However, their work is not the heart of the relevant business. Hospitals and the media are interesting in the way that their core business is the same as that of the professionals they employ. The difference between hospitals and the media is that this is taken for granted rather than downplayed as inconvenient.

Risk, Not Wrongdoing, the Reason for Ethic and Regulation in General (and Ethics Regimes in Particular)

Those seeking legal or ethical regulation of the media are often met with flat denials that any problem exists. They may be asked to prove that media corporations have misused their capacity to influence public opinion such as favoring particular candidates, supporting certain policies, or taking a particular line on their show. Such actions are difficult to prove because they will not, of their nature, be transparent and open.

Just as media owners have interests to protect, so do politicians. There is strong evidence of problems in the recent past. According to Chadwick (1989), the policies pursued by the former Prime Minister Bob Hawke's Labor government were motivated by the government's political interests. More recently, in evidence before a 1994 Senate committee hearing, media baron Conrad Black complained that another former Australian Prime Minister, Paul Keating, made a deal—a rise to 35% ownership if political coverage for the then forthcoming 1993 election was even handed.

On the influence of international media owners, Black again condemned himself unwittingly. Black claimed that he only once interfered with the editorial line of the *Daily Telegraph.* When President Reagan bombed Libya (including an attack on Colonel Gaddafy's tent), England provided bases, and other European countries objected, with France denying overflight rights. The action was blatantly illegal under international law (indeed, it was later revealed that the bombing for which this was a public reprisal was carried out from Syria). The *Telegraph* made this point rather gently. Black thought that this was obviously wrong. The merits of this argument are not at stake at this moment. Whatever the rights and wrongs on such an issue, the views of North Americans should not determine the editorials of English newspapers on matters of sovereignty, international law, and armed conflict.

On the relationship between media owners and their other interests, the liaison between Alan Bond and Joh Bjelke Petersen is a classic case. Bjelke Petersen sued Channel 9 for alleging some improprieties in his administration. Alan Bond went to sort it out. According to Bond, Bjelke made it clear that life would be extremely difficult for Bond's brewing interests if he did not settle. Settlement was very expensive—especially given the apparent view of Bond's own lawyers and the enormous embarrassment that a vigorously fought defense might cause to Bjelke at that time. Bond paid $400,000 and discovered that Queensland gave him no trouble at all. They made a deal that benefitted them both but at the expense of ordinary citizens. As participants in democracy, we were lumbered with a regime whose flaws were not fully exposed until later in the decade. As participants in the market, we suffered the inefficiencies of privileged access to governmental favor.

Yet, a demand for proof of current or future wrongdoing misses the point of an ethics regime for the media industry. All that must be demonstrated is that there is a temptation to misuse the capacity of media organizations and media participants to influence public opinion for their own benefit. If there is the temptation, there is the risk that mere mortals will succumb to it.

A government does not have to prove that another country is planning to invade before it establishes a defense force. A corporation does not wait for a fire before installing fire alarms. It does not even have to prove there is a risk before taking such preventative measures. It identifies, manages, and avoids the risk—at the same time taking out insurance as a means of dealing with disaster should it occur.

The media industry should not
wait until standards are breached
and punitive measures are
required before taking preventive
action.

If we are to protect our democracy, we must deal with the risks that might compromise it. Thus, the media industry should not wait until standards are breached and punitive measures are required before taking preventive action. There will always be risks wherever there is a potential conflict of interest, especially at the interface between the institutions of democracy and the mechanism of the market. What is required of both media regulators and media organizations is to identify those risks and develop robust risk management strategies. An ethics regime should be seen as part of a sound risk management policy for the media industry and the polity it is intended to serve.

Elements of an Ethic
and Integrity Regime for the Media

Ethical Standard Setting, Legal Regulation, and Institutional Reform—The Essential Trinity for an Ethics Regime

How can we deal with this risk? There are three kinds of responses: legal, ethical, and institutional. The overwhelming preference is for establishing ethical standards that emphasize character and rely on modifying the conduct of individuals.[4] This preference was reflected in the number of papers presented at the International Media Ethics Conference in Canberra where many speakers advocated virtue ethics as the key to recovering media credibility. For Jay Black, Simon Longstaff, and Cratis Hippocrates, encouraging the moral character and autonomy of individual journalists is the key to media ethics.[5] Self-regulation and ethical codes are partial responses to the decline in media credibility. Sampford (1994, 2002) has long argued that individual ethics without institutional ethics and legal backing is insufficient and indeed, neither is adequate by itself.[6]

Ethics codes are a part of the answer but not all of it. What is needed is an ethics regime that includes a set of ethical standards but also includes a number of legal and institutional means to realize those standards. A bare code of ethics without the support of laws that impose sanctions will become a "knaves charter"—a guide for the good and a dead letter for the bad. In other words, Klaidman and Beauchamp's (1987) "virtuous journalist" who is committed to honesty, integrity, fairness, and accountability needs an environment that supports and nurtures such virtues. An ethics regime can contribute to this aspiration by supporting and going beyond a professional code of ethics. Similarly, law that is disconnected from the values of those it seeks to regulate may fail for lack of ethical support. However, an ethics regime is not just legal and ethical rules. Even the best coordinated set of mutually reinforcing ethical and legal rules can be undermined if those who are supposed to be guided by those rules work within unsupportive institutions where they are faced with conflicting demands or temptations to act unethically. Standards need to be built into the industry as a whole and into the organizational and management structures of the organizations to which they apply. Hence, we have argued that coordinated ethical standard setting, legal regulation, and institutional reform are essential in promoting higher standards of conduct and dealing with those whose conduct falls below the acceptable.

Moving Beyond Minimum Compliance

We emphasize that the purposes of an ethics regime are more than just preventing unacceptable behavior. Creating rules and agencies that simply receive and adjudicate complaints and sanction breaches does help to establish minimum standards of conduct, especially where the sanctions have real teeth, including the suspension or removal of a professional license to practice or a government license to broadcast. However, it offers no incentive to move beyond those standards and may give the false impression that meeting minimum standards is all ethics is about. People might see themselves as ethical merely because they comply with the minimum standards for practice within their profession or industry. So long as an existing or potential licensee is not seen as falling below the lowest common denominator in the industry, ethical issues can be ignored. Worse, there is often an uneasy suspicion that licenses and benefits are given to media organizations because of subtle threats to use media power against a government if it does not concede to the organization's demands. Rather than rewarding media organizations for acting ethically, there is often a perception that media organizations are rewarded because they threaten to act unethically.

There is often a perception that media organizations are rewarded because they threaten to act unethically.

An ethics regime should encourage industry participants to look beyond minimum standards and encourage them to match and surpass the highest standards of the profession or industry. Instead of rewarding those who threaten to act unethically, licensing systems should reward those who make the most credible promises to act in the interest of the wider community and for the public good and to strive for ethical excellence. Those seeking licenses and other benefits should show that they recognize the dilemmas and temptations (i.e., risks) in the modern media industry and come up with substantive suggestions as to how they will manage them. Those organizations that demonstrate a capacity to manage and avoid such risks should be viewed as more appropriate licensees. If the representatives of a democratic polity are to hand over public assets like broadcast bandwidth to media organizations, they should hand them over to those who are least likely to abuse the power that such assets give them. This offers the hope of a virtuous competition and ethical innovation among the companies in the improvement of ethical and governance processes.

This is not a distortion of the system for allocating licenses. It simply draws into the equation another extremely relevant factor and allows for a financially advantageous bid to be trumped by a bid that includes a more credible ethics regime. We emphasize that this is not a new factor. In addition to any personal moral reasons we may have for acting ethically, the integrity of news media is an important social and political asset. The introduction of ethics does not complicate the choices faced by media proprietors. It merely reinforces some reasons for choices and weakens others. In the same way as licensing regimes can support corporate ethics by providing rewards for good ethics regimes, media organizations should in turn recognize and reward those members of staff who behave ethically.

A theme that appeared consistently during the 2002 Media Ethics Conference in Canberra is the apparent tension between upholding the public interest and being profitable. Many presenters identified a clash between the notion of the role of the media as the fourth estate and the market ideologies that operate in the industry. At the conference, Stuart Longstaff asserted that the pursuit of profits overrides the pursuit of public interest, and the language of ethics is more about public relations than any depth of commitment to ethical values and conduct. Similarly, Ian Richards questioned the plausibility of journalism ethics in a world of corporate journalism.

We argue that maintaining ethical standards does not have to threaten the economic gains. Regulation does not have to be hostile to commercial interests. An ethics regime with the appropriate incentives can align both objectives. An effective regime can create a mutually supportive environment for the pursuit of public interest and profit. In the current climate of public cynicism and mistrust of media practices and standards, the industry needs to see ethics as the best policy for long-term success. Maintaining social trust is an important part of ethical conduct and credibility. Media proprietors and journalists know that there is a great deal to lose if the media are seen as just another commercial activity divorced from the status and responsibility attributed to them as the fourth estate. This idea, although tarnished, remains resilient within the media industry.

A Range of Standards and a Standard to Be Raised

One of the most common mistakes in designing codes of conduct is to frame them in the following form.

Rule 1: Every journalist, doctor, or lawyer will act according to the highest standards of the profession.

Rule 2: Anyone who breaches Rule 1 is guilty of a breach of this code and liable to disqualification.

If taken literally, this would shrink all professions to a single practitioner. There can only be one person who is subject to the highest standards. Therefore, everybody else is in breach of Rule 1 and liable to be expelled under Rule 2.

A code of conduct or ethics needs an "aspirational" component that sets the highest standards to which a profession might aspire. Not everyone will achieve that standard. Thus, any code of ethics needs to recognize a range of relevant standards:

- Below the aspirational apex of performance lies the standard of "good practice" that indicates a high level of professional performance that deserves to be rewarded.
- Below good practice lies "acceptable practice"—good enough to remain in practice and/or retain a license.
- Below that lies "dubious practice," the acceptability of which is questionable and that may make it hard to keep down a job.
- Below that lie the various levels of substandard behavior that produce sanctions—from a reduced opportunity for development, to loss of license, to criminal sanctions.

These levels of standards should not be isolated but coordinated. Thus, the disciplinary standards are clearly seen as the negation of the aspirational standards, and those who keep their eyes on the highest standards of the profession do not fall foul of the disciplinary ones. The explicit aim of any ethics and integrity regime is to raise the standard of as many professionals as possible—to as near the aspirational goal as possible and as far as possible above the level that attracts discipline. Interestingly, this renders less likely that behavior will occur that is in contravention of the minimum standards. Further, there is generally less sympathy for perpetrators, and whistle-blowers are more secure. In other words, we are proposing a comprehensive and integrative ethics regime.

The Value of Codes

Journalists—and many political theorists, including John Keane (1991)—have long recognized that their critical role in the formation of public opinion in a democracy imposes ethical obligations on them. However, there are others in the media, including talk show hosts, with an equally instrumental role in the formation of public opinion. The issue is whether all media practitioners have ethical obligations arising out of the part they play in the formation of public opinion, what those obligations are, and how they are enforced.

How to define those ethical obligations? It would be a mistake merely to extend the journalists' code of ethics to those whose activities overlap journalism in form and/or function. It is better to establish ethics regimes that specifically address the ethical issues raised by different kinds of work. In this regard, we argue very strongly that all in the media who contribute to the formation of public opinion should be involved in the process of formulating and enforcing such codes of ethics.

A more specific example of coordinating such codes can be found in the public services of Queensland and Western Australia. In both cases, a general aspirational code has been established for the public service as a whole—that is, a statement of the ideals to which a public servant should aspire. Under the umbrella of the aspirational code, "agency-specific" codes—interpretations of those ideals for public servants in the specific agencies—are developed. Whereas a service-wide code is too general to be enforceable as such, agency-specific codes can provide the basis for disciplinary codes.

A similar general aspirational code could be devised for the media—or at least for those parts of the media involved in the formation of public opinion. At the heart of aspirational codes are the raison d'être or the "justification" of a professional activity. Any profession or organization needs to justify itself to the community of which it is a part. These justifications are particularly important for those who seek particular privileges not possessed by others (e.g., for journalists' protection of journalistic freedom). Doctors justify themselves in promoting the health of the community, lawyers in promoting the rule of law, and police in terms of reducing the level of crime. Joint stock companies justify themselves on the basis that they increase the prosperity of the community by concentrating resources and talent in a way that not only increases the wealth of shareholders but benefits consumers by providing goods and services at competitive prices and benefits employees by giving them alternative avenues for employment at better rates than would be found in less developed economic structures. For the media, the justifications are based on a claimed capacity to entertain and also to assist in the transmission of ideas and information to assist citizens in taking part in the cultural and political life of the community. It is on the basis of fulfilling those needs that media organizations should, and generally do, grow and become profitable.

Such a justification allows the coordination of the three essential elements of an ethics regime. It provides the principles that assist the interpretation of the legislation and regulations applying to that industry. It provides the normative basis for the institution's ethics and the positive standards by which the professionals should judge themselves and be judged. Finally, it provides a standard for analysis and review of the institutional design and functioning of media organizations.

The general media-wide aspirational code is then available to provide the bases for more specific codes for the individual organizations and professions that make up the media. These are

- Codes for different types of media industries—e.g., broadcasting, TV, print, and Internet. These would in turn be interpreted to apply to individual media organizations depending on audience and format.
- Codes for different professions within the industry—e.g., journalists, talk show hosts, broadcasters, public relations practitioners, and management.

Each is an interpretation of the general aspirational code to the particular circumstances of different professional groups and different media organizations. Each should also consider the particular temptations and dilemmas thrown up by their daily work and provide guidance in handling those temptations and dilemmas.

Moving Beyond Mere Rules and Codes—To an Ethics Regime or "Integrity System" for the Media

To back up these codes and make them effective, legal rules and institutional supports need to be created or enlivened. We do not have enough time to detail them here. However, we would recommend the following.

Legal Reform to Support These Codes

Laws should include those that (a) provide legal sanctions for conduct that falls below that which is set in the disciplinary elements of the codes, (b) protect whistle-blowers who report breaches, and (c) strengthen corporate governance requirements.

The aim of an integrity regime is to fix the eyes of media personnel on the highest standards in the profession so that they remain sufficiently above the minimum standards and so that they will never fall foul of them. To achieve this, however, it is necessary to coordinate the laws that impose sanctions with the aspirational codes of ethics.

Sanctions should definitely include license cancellation. This has often seemed too dramatic and damaging to the interests of other shareholders; however, this is where good corporate governance can come to the rescue. If the rules are set out clearly in advance, the board is able to evaluate the risk and install a risk-management strategy. If the value of their main asset is likely to be put at risk by a decision or policy of the board, the board is duty bound to avoid approving actions that might realize that risk. If the majority shareholder were to seek to influence the editorial policy to assist his other interests, that would involve a very substantial conflict of interest, which the other directors should never tolerate. Similarly, a proprietor who sought to influence the editorial content of the paper would again be facing a conflict of interest.

Organization-Specific Institutional Components

These fall into two main categories:

1. Organization-specific institutional components, which include ethics committees and an incentives system (for ethical action).
2. System wide institutions, which include a Media Integrity Commissioner (IC), a Media Integrity Council (MIC), and licensing bodies for the various media services that require a license.

Ethics committees.   We recommend that these include staff from all levels of an organization. Functions to be allocated would be as follows:

- Assisting in the development of the organization's code.
- Monitoring the development of the organization's code.
- Advising on difficult issues as they arise.

- Providing a source of advice to individual media professionals outside the chain of command.

Incentive structures. These need to be designed to ensure that they support rather than undermine ethical conduct. They need the following:

- Requirement of evidence of high standards of ethical behavior in promotions and appointments.
- Requirement of evidence of such standards in general awards.
- Awards for the most ethically aware media agency.

Media Integrity Commissioner

A commissioner would fulfill the following functions:

- Develop ethics-awareness programs.
- Assist with the process of drafting codes.
- Ethics coordination: Coordinating approaches to improve conduct through different mechanisms.
- Provide a central source of ethics advice: A body to whom the agency in-house advisers could turn when they are uncertain.
- Advise on any newly proposed management processes to ensure that they further rather than retard high ethical standards. New management processes seem to emerge every few years, and it is important to know if there are unintended consequences.
- Monitoring of the ethics processes within the media: Receiving reports and recommending action to Parliament, the Australian Competition and Consumer Commission, the Australian Broadcasting Authority (ABA), or other bodies with the power or influence to improve the process.
- Ethics research, including the following: (a) monitoring international best practice and communicating such to agencies; (b) research into source of problems (this feeds into risk assessment, policy, code development, and reporting); (c) promoting and frequently providing ethics education and training; ethics education is essential in making an ethics regime effective. However, it can also provide some useful case studies for research and policy development.
- Ethical audits (or risk assessments): To anticipate potential ethical failures within media organizations in general or particular kinds of programs in particular. These could be followed up with advice on how to handle the risks that were identified.

The IC would have a crucial role to play. He or she would help to drive the whole process and would assist in its development, maintenance, and improvement. However, the IC would not have power to investigate complaints (such a role would be in conflict with the IC's role in providing advice).[7]

MIC

This body would provide an advisory board whose function would be to advise the IC in the exercise of the IC's functions. It would also advise on the most difficult issues coming to the IC and to institutional ethics committees. It would perform a function similar to the Human Ethics Committee of Australia's National Health and Medical Research Council and other bodies playing similar roles in other countries in setting guidelines for institutional ethics committees.

Licensing Bodies

The existing licensing bodies would continue to make decisions on whether licenses should be issued and/or withdrawn. In addition to their usual license hearing, the licensing bodies should approve the codes put to them for validation and endorsement. It would also include an ethics investigation body. They should be independent of the IC and would provide individual investigations of possible wrongdoing.

Constitutional Constraints

One of the problems of regulating the media in Australia has been the lack of Commonwealth power over the press. Section 51 (v) of the Australian Constitution gives it power over "postal, telegraphic, telephonic; and other like services" (see www.aph.gov.au). This has been extended since 1935 (*R v. Brislan*) to include radio and later television. Yet there has never been a basis for regulation of the press. However, with the growing integration of the media and its reliance on electronic forms of delivery, any media corporation that uses these electronic forms could be covered by Commonwealth legislation.

Implementation

Implementation of a comprehensive ethics and integrity regime would be a major exercise. We suggest the following as a broad set of procedures for implementation.

1. Appoint a Media Ethics Commissioner, Staff, and Media Ethics Committee.

2. Undertake an overall ethics audit of the Australian media to identify problems that need to be dealt with.

3. Develop an industry-wide aspirational ethics code.

4. Develop broad industry-wide, ethics-awareness programs. Initial sessions would educate staff on the nature of ethics, discuss ethical issues they have had to face, and inform staff of some of the means of institutionalizing ethics in the workplace.

5. Develop ethics committees in individual media corporations. These would provide input and feedback. It is recommended that in some cases, smaller groups ("ethical circles") be formed.

6. Develop justification statements for each media outlet. Here, staff consider the values that justify the media organization, first in ethical circles then through the ethics committees.

7. Draft general codes for individual organizations based on the values that justify it.

8. Draft specific codes for individual organizations. This will generally include both aspirational and disciplinary elements (although the latter may end up included in formal rules, policies, and contractual responsibilities).

9. Develop ongoing monitoring and educational structures within both the office of the Media Integrity Commissioner and the individual organizations.

Objections: Profitability and Capital Flight

Two objections are often raised against integrity and governance improvements: the effect on profitability and the possibility that media organizations might leave the country.

Profitability. We argue that none of these measures stops a media company from making a profit. The commercial imperatives still operate in seeking audiences. Where there is a niche of opinion that is not catered for, there will be opportunities to fill it. Things that would remain problematic include cash for comment, advertising for editorial, and political support for other benefits to their economic interests. If this makes media investments less attractive for those who would seek to profit through those means, then we make no apologies. If any media players announce that they bought in believing that they could use media assets for those purposes, we will apologize that they have been misled, ask who it is who has misled them, and refer both to the federal police as well as suggesting that the rest of their affairs might be profitably examined! Of course, no one will admit to such motivations, so we can ignore the complaint and quietly hail their departure as they slink away. With the departure of those who are in media for such nonmedia reasons, it will make room for those who want to profit from selling people information and ideas. It will reduce the value of media assets to the extent that others wanted to misuse them. On the other hand, it will increase their value as true media assets. Most important, it will prevent the value and reputation of them as media assets being compromised by the owners' other agendas.

Capital flight. One of the most common arguments against the setting of standards in corporate governance or accountability is that companies will flee to the least regulated jurisdiction. Some might even argue that some of Australia's media corporations would be uncomfortable with a requirement for higher ethical standards and higher ethical requirements. We would like to think that all our media companies would welcome higher ethical standards and claim that they already exceed them. Even if this is a bit optimistic, if a media corporation were to seek to locate offshore following an increase in ethical requirements, this would not enhance its reputation. In fact, integrity avoidance might ultimately be more damaging to its reputation than tax avoidance!

Integrity is more important for media with news or quasi-news functions than for most other industries. If Australia were to establish itself as "an island of integrity" through a strong and credible ethics regime, media organizations that subjected themselves to that regime could claim greater credibility. Not only would Australian media organizations be inclined to stay, others might seek to gain the seal of approval.

Finally, if Australian media outlets are to be long-term global brands, they will have to satisfy other people that they will not act to compromise democracy in their country. If they adopt means by which people can be confident that their democracies are not threatened, it would be sensible for them to prefer Australian media companies. (There is an argument that such compromises are exactly what some leaders of other countries want. However, although this approach might make it difficult to do business in some dictatorships, it will stand them in good stead when those countries cease to be dictatorships.)

Concentration of Media Ownership
and Cross-Media Ownership

The approach taken here is to use an ethics and integrity regime to minimize the likelihood that the power that comes from the media's role in the formation of public opinion will be abused. This is different from the traditional approach of minimizing the power of each proprietor by insisting on diversity of ownership. Although there are other reasons for retaining diversity, some of the reasons for it can be diminished with the development of a media-integrity system. If there were a trade-off between a strong ethics regime and some further acceptance of cross-media ownership, we would unequivocally favor the former.

Recent Legislative Proposals

In this light, the proposed reforms in the 2002 Broadcasting Services Amendment (Media Ownership) Bill[8] showed some promise despite some huge flaws. The more positive aspects include an unwinding of supposed protections provided by Australian ownership and diversity of that ownership. They also involve a small step in the general direction suggested by getting media companies seeking takeover authorization to outline their plans, rules, and structures avoiding a mischief to which diversity of ownership was directed. However, the provisions are very weak. Most important, they do not address the main reason why diversity of media ownership is argued, most famously by media mogul Rupert Murdoch in the 1960s.

The bill proposes an editorial-separation system as the key mechanism to preserve diversity. However, it ignores one of the long-standing reasons for media diversity (once championed by Rupert Murdoch)—that different owners would have different views. It does nothing to prevent those with expanded media ownership from exercising it to influence or even direct their expanded media empires. The requirement of providing basic information on editorial policy cannot fulfill that function and is not designed to do so. It says, "Lord Beaverbrook, you are welcome."

At the same time, the means by which exemptions from cross-media and foreign ownership rules may be granted are fraught with another danger. Decisions are up to ministers rather than an independent body. Although foreign investments are vetted by the Foreign Investments Review Board (FIRB), and recommendations are made to the minister, the governance issues outlined here are not part of the FIRB's current brief and culture. In any case, they will not be privy to the discussions between media companies and ministers. When it comes to cross-media rules, there is no such independent body.

In their current form, the proposed changes increase the risk of corruption. In some hands, it would be a recipe for corruption. We have already alluded to past incidences of liaisons between media proprietors and politicians. What is to stop future media owners consummating the kind of deal that Conrad Black claimed he had with Paul Keating—and Bond claimed he had with Bjelke? (Indeed, it might be worse than Black and Keating. Without the need for legislative change and the power in the hands of relevant ministers, the minister would have no excuse for holding off.) At the moment, there are numerous politicians all people can think of but few of us would name whom none of us could trust with this kind of power. The point is not whether this or that minister or proprietor is good or bad. The point is whether we give them a temptation to such corrupt deals. These proposals increase the incentive and reduce the scrutiny. We ask, rhetorically, is this a risk we should consider acceptable?

> *As media ownership becomes concentrated, an elite few have substantial influence with an important element of democracy: information.*

As media ownership becomes concentrated, an elite few have substantial influence with an important element of democracy: information. The media constitute a power elite. Managing the use and abuse of that power is a principle concern. If Australian ownership and diversity of that ownership are to be abandoned, effective ethics and integrity regimes are essential. However, if people can ensure the development and implementation of an effective ethics and integrity regime, such changes have potential merit. We are not opposed to the general thrust and the substitution of formal structures in place of ownership diversity as a means of preserving the ability of the media to perform their democratic functions.

Political Considerations

It would be unwise to attack those media organizations that are in the industry for profit alone. Although it would be unethical for such organizations to use the media to attack reforms that would compel them to be more ethical, it would not, of course, be surprising. Indeed, it would not be surprising if such media organizations offered their support to a political party in return for its opposing these reforms. Even if they did not do so, the risk would have a chilling effect on any one political party. This is why bipartisan agreement would be extremely important, possibly crucial. If both parties agreed to refuse to modify the policy despite promises of assistance at the next election, such inducements lose their sting. Indeed, if the parties agreed to publicize any such approaches, this would effectively deter attempts at such inducements and also make the point of why the reforms are needed.

This is one of those areas in which political parties need to recognize that giving in to such pressure or the risk of such pressure is a dangerous strategy. Each time a party gives something away to a media organization for favorable coverage, it does three things:

1. Increases the effective power of the media organization.
2. Whets its appetite.
3. Skews the media in favor of those who would do such deals against those who would not.

This might seem a clever short-term tactic. However, it damages the long-term interests of that party and weakens the future effectiveness of the government offices its members seek to win. This is why we would like to see both major parties engage in a "virtuous conspiracy" to improve the effectiveness of the media in our democracy and make life difficult for those who would undercut democracy. In doing so, they will also do a great favor to the media, business, and themselves.

Conclusions

An important function of the media is to provide citizens with information that will empower them to make informed political choices. The basis of democracy is not simply one vote per citizen but an informed vote. The media are a critical element of an effective democracy because they are the principle means by which citizens receive the information and the cocktail of views that allow them to choose how they exercise their votes. The media also have a critical watchdog role without which few national integrity systems could function. These functions are worth protecting and promoting. Having said that, the activities of the media can have positive and negative effects on peoples' understanding of public issues. Those working in the media industry have better access to information and other resources—technological and organizational. The media professionals have considerable freedom to gather and disseminate information. However, not all them use their liberty sagaciously. Moreover, the concentration of such privileges in the hands of a few global media proprietors poses a risk to democratic governance. It is, therefore, in peoples' interest to develop a regulatory regime that minimizes the risk that this power will be misused and that ministers will be tempted to make deals in return for that misuse and at the same time maximizes the chance that the media will use this power to fulfill the critical functions of the media in a democracy.

The ethics regime being proposed takes a coordinated, comprehensive, and holistic approach that involves the formulation and implementation of regulatory ideals and mechanisms at multiple levels and domains of activities—from voluntary forms of self-regulation such as ethics codes to more interventionist strategies such as government regulations. A media ethics regime will contain prescriptive and proscriptive aspects identifying what is required, what is prohibited, and how to achieve those ends; a disciplinary aspect linking breaches with sanctions; an educative aspect teaching what is expected of the members of the profession; a merit or reward aspect recognizing and encouraging ethical excellence; and finally, an aspirational aspect going beyond basic or minimal requirements to affirming ideals. This ethics regime is predominantly preventive in character and is the core of a key risk-management strategy for the protection of democracy.

Notes

1. The existing regulatory mechanisms for the media industry are largely ad hoc, idiosyncratic, and with uneven levels of control. The legal basis of regulation of each sector of the media industry is different—the Commonwealth's power over the print media flows from its constitutionally more limited ability to make laws over interstate and international trade and its corporate affairs powers. The print media are subjected to general provisions of the Trade Practices Act. The Australian Press Council is a self-regulatory, compliants-based body. There is no independent regulatory authority. The broadcasting media enjoy less self-regulation than the print media. They are subjected to high-level regulation of a lease system that comes under the Broadcasting Services Act 1992. Commercial broadcasting media are subject to the scrutiny of the ABA, which allocates and reviews licences, investigates complaints, and generally defines what is adequate provision of service to the community.

2. These recommendations are based on the best ethics and governance practice in the government and corporate sectors and on the latest international thinking on how that practice might be developed and enhanced. They incorporate ideas that emerged out of the Fitzgerald and "WA Inc" enquiries and their aftermath and from the Nolan Committee (which made recommendations for integrity mechanisms after the "cash for questions" scandal in the United Kingdom). In particular, they draw on the OECD's recommendations for ethics and integrity systems, which in turn derive from the work cited previously. They also draw on some of the recommendations to BHP for its ethics and integrity system, under development since the beginning of the decade.

3. For analyses of the "Cash for Comment" scandal, see Gordon-Smith (2002) "Media Ethics After 'Cash for Comment'"; Johnson (2000)

Cash for Comment: The Seduction of Journo Culture; and Overington (1999) "John Laws: Show Me the Money."

4. This is abundant in research on individual ethics, journalistic codes, guidelines, and ideals of journalistic responsibility in mass communication and journalism studies. For example see, Christians, Ferré, and Fackler (1993) *Good News: A Social Ethics of the Press;* Elliott (1986) *Responsible Journalism;* Klaidman and Beauchamp (1987) *The Virtuous Journalist;* Lambeth (1992) *Committed Journalism;* and Meyer (1987) *Ethical Journalism.*

5. Jay Black (2002) held the Poynter–Jamison Chair in Media Ethics, University of South Florida St. Petersburg. Simon Longstaff is the Executive Director of St. James Ethics Centre, Sydney, New South Wales, Australia. Cratis Hippocrates was Group Editorial Learning & Development Manager of John Fairfax Holdings, Sydney, New South Wales, Australia.

6. See Sampford (2002) "Institutionalising Public Sector Ethics" and Sampford (1994) "Law, Ethics and Institutional Design: Finding Philosophy, Displacing Ideology."

7. For a discussion of the critical role of giving advice on ethical issues, see Sampford (2001) "Prior Advice Is Better Than Subsequent Investigation."

8. To date, this has been blocked in the Senate. The government has not retreated from its desire to have these reforms passed and may seek to have them enacted after the next election.

References

Belsey, A., & Chadwick, R. (1999). Ethics as a vehicle for media quality. In R. M. Baird, W. E. Loges, & S. E. Rosenbaum (Eds.), *The media and morality* (pp. 65–67). New York: Prometheus Books.

Black, J. (2002). Teaching—and doing—media ethics with a high grip on reality. *Australian Journal of Professional and Applied Ethics,* 4(2), pp. 48–55.

Chadwick, P. (1989). *Media mates. Carving Up Australia's Media.* Melbourne, Victoria, Australia: Macmillan.

Christians, C., Ferré, J., & Fackler, M. (1993). *Good news: A social ethics of the press.* New York: Oxford University Press.

Elliott, D. (Ed.). (1986). *Responsible journalism.* Newbury Park, CA: Sage.

Gordon-Smith, M. (2002). Media ethics after "Cash for Comment." In S. Cunningham & G. Turner (Eds.), *The media and communications in Australia.* Sydney, Australia: Allen & Unwin.

Johnson, R. (2000). *Cash for comment: The seduction of journo culture.* Annandale, New South Wales, Australia: Pluto Press.

Keane, J. (1991). *The media and democracy.* Cambridge, England: Polity Press.

Klaidman, S., & Beauchamp, T. L. (1987). *The virtuous journalist.* New York: Oxford University Press.

Lambeth, E. B. (1992). *Committed journalism* (2nd ed.). Bloomington: Indiana University Press.

Meyer, P. (1987). *Ethical journalism.* New York: Longman.

Overington, C. (1999, July 17). John Laws: Show me the money. *The Age,* p. 1.

R v. Brislan, ex parte Williams (1935) 54 CLR 262.

Sampford, C. (1994). Institutionalising public sector ethics. In N. Preston (Ed.), *Ethics for the public sector: Education training* (p. 114). Sydney, Australia: Federation Press.

Sampford, C. (2001). Prior advice is better than subsequent investigation. In J. Fleming & I. Holland (Eds.), *Motivating ministers to morality* (pp. 173–186). Aldershot, England: Ashgate.

Sampford, C. (2002). Institutionalising public sector ethics. In D. Elliott (Ed.), *Encyclopedia of life support systems* (pp. 573–590). Oxford, England: EOLSS Publishers Co.

Journal of Mass Media Ethics, 19(2), 108–118
Copyright © 2004, Lawrence Erlbaum Associates, Inc.

Good Character:
Too Little, Too Late

Neil Levy
University of Melbourne

❑ *The influence of virtue theory is spreading to the professions. I argue that journalists and educators would do well to refrain from placing too much faith in the power of the virtues to guide working journalists. Rather than focus on the character of the journalist, we would do better to concentrate on institutional constraints on unethical conduct. I urge this position in the light of the critique of virtue ethics advanced, especially, by Gilbert Harman (1999). Harman believed that the empirical findings of psychologists show that character-based approaches to ethics are useless. I suspect that this rather overstates the case. Nevertheless, special features of journalism make virtue-centered approaches especially inappropriate, and we had best turn to alternatives.*

What Is Virtue Ethics and Why Is Everyone
Talking About It?

Consequentialism and rights-based approaches to ethics, still the best known moral theories, focus directly on the notion of right action. Consequentialism provides a positive theory of right action. It tells us that everyone is to do that action that, of the alternatives open to them, maximizes utility (or whatever other good it aims at). Rights-based theories provide a negative account of right action. That is, they do not dictate a unique course of action to agents but instead place constraints on what they may do. Whatever they do, they must not violate anyone's rights.

Virtue ethics is crucially different from both these approaches. Rather than focus on action, it concentrates on character. It exhorts everyone to cultivate the virtues: those excellences of character that are the possession of the ideally virtuous person. Virtue ethics therefore only provides action guidance in a derivative manner. Rather than telling people that they ought to maximize utility or refrain from rights violations, it tells them to behave honestly, compassionately, and so on (and, correlatively, that they ought not to behave dishonestly, callously, etc.). Proponents of virtue ethics claim that this is a more humane vision of morality than that presented by its rivals. It does not place excessive demands on people by asking them to behave in a counterintuitive fashion, as deontology and consequentialism notoriously can, and it does not ask them to guide their lives by alien principles and rules. It is, in fact, more attuned to the phenomenology of prereflective moral experience. It does not ask people to replace everyday morality with a theoretical system that is alleged to improve on it; instead, it introduces a system into that prereflective morality. Finally, it alone can account for the fact that morality is as much a matter of motivation as of belief, and it alone gives a central place to the practical wisdom and judgment that agents need to act well in difficult circumstances.

Virtue ethics has been particularly attractive to people interested in delineating the ethics of the professions. Professional ethics has been dominated by so-called role morality, which holds that professionals ought to act in a manner appropriate to their function as professionals, to the roles they play in society, rather than be guided directly by more universalistic concerns. Virtue ethics, as it is usually understood, is not role morality because the virtues to which it appeals are understood to be valid for everyone no matter what position they occupy in society. Nevertheless, role morality and virtue ethics seem natural allies, the more so because role morality can be spelled out by asking professionals to cultivate the character traits that enable them to perform their tasks. Moreover, at least one influential formulation of virtue ethics, that of Alasdair MacIntyre (1985), appeals directly to social roles to ground the virtues. For MacIntyre (1985), a virtue is an acquired trait that allows its possessor to achieve the goods that are internal to a particular practice; a practice, in turn, is defined as

> Any coherent and complex form of socially established cooperative human activity through which goods internal to that form of activity are realized in the course of trying to achieve those standards of excellence which are appropriate to, and partially definitive of, that form of activity, with the result that human powers to achieve excellence, and human conceptions of the ends and goods involved, are systematically extended. (p. 198)

Obviously, on this view, virtues are closely tied to roles. Any practice in which human excellences are extended in a distinctive manner is an appropriate locus for the exercise of the virtues, and the virtues are those qualities that allow practitioners to excel in their roles.

Ethicists and reflective practitioners concerned with the best approach to the problems that confront journalists have been as quick as anyone else to embrace virtue ethics (Klaidman & Beauchamp, 1987; Lambeth, 1990; Belsey, 1998; Borden, 1999). The best known example here is Klaidman and Beauchamp's book whose title is self-explanatory: *The Virtuous Journalist.* For its authors, journalists, first and foremost, ought to be guided by excellences of character, which will enable them to behave properly in all the difficult situations they confront in the course of their work. If society ensures that its journalists are virtuous, it will need relatively little in the way of regulation to ensure that their conduct will be ethical. Journalists will not need to be cajoled into doing the right thing nor threatened with punishment if they fail to comply. Instead, virtuous journalism will be a matter of course for them. Kaidman and Beauchamp (1987) maintained everyone shall all benefit from this state of affairs, noting that "the public is better served when journalists perform well because of good character than because of sanctions, threats, rules, laws, regulations, and the like" (p. 18).

Rather than focus on principles, rights, rules, or legislation, society should ensure that journalists are of good character. Journalistic education should focus on inculcating the virtues appropriate to the profession.

What virtues ought journalists to display? Klaidman and Beauchamp (1987) did not attempt to provide an exhaustive list, but they did provide the beginnings of a catalogue: "Virtues like fairness, truthfulness, trustworthiness, and non-malevolence (avoiding harm) come to mind" (p. 19). I shall not attempt to evaluate this list. Instead, I shall concentrate on just one item on it. If anything counts as a virtue for the journalist, surely honesty must. On an account such as MacIntyre's (1985), according to which a virtue is a character trait that allows its possessor to realize the goals of a particular practice, honesty will certainly count as a virtue of the journalist. If journalism has a goal, it is the production of truth. According to the fourth estate model of the media, their aim is to provide the public with information that will enable it to elect a government that represents its interests and to act as a watchdog guarding against abuses of power both public and private. Both these functions require the production of truth: truth concerning what politicians say and do, concerning the behavior of business and bureaucracy, and so on.[1] Honesty is obviously a virtue conducive to the production and dissemination of truth. News reports must be truthful and must be known to be truthful, or the public will not in fact be informed by them. To this end, journalists must be honest and known to be honest.

> *Focusing on the character of the*
> *journalist will not be an effective*
> *way of producing honest*
> *journalism.*

Thus honesty is the, or at least a, paradigm virtue for journalists, which is to say that if anything counts as a virtue for the profession, it must. If, therefore, it is doubtful that the creation of honest journalists is an effective way of ensuring ethical behavior in journalism, the whole enterprise of virtue ethics in the service of journalism will be fatally undermined. This is precisely the claim I here defend: Focusing on the character of the journalist will not be an effective way of producing honest journalism.

The Situationist Critique of Virtue Ethics

Very recently, virtue ethics has come under sustained criticism from a number of philosophers who claim that it is empirically inadequate. These thinkers point to the results of a number of well-known psychological experiments that demonstrate, they claim, that there is no such thing as character. Most famous of all these experiments is that conducted by Stanley Milgram (1974). Milgram's participants were told that they were to participate in a study of the effects of punishment on learning. They were introduced to another person who, they were told, was another volunteer. Then they drew lots to see who would be the learner and who the teacher. The learner had electrodes attached to him. His or her task was to memorize word pairs, which the teacher then asked him or her to recall. If he or she made a mistake (or failed to answer at all), he or she was given an electric shock. The first shock was set for 15 V; with each subsequent shock, the intensity increased by 15 V up to 450 V.

In actual fact, this elaborate apparatus, the entire experiment, was fake. The other participant was really an accomplice of Milgram's (1974), and his or her failures to recall word pairs were deliberate. No shocks were administered to him or her; instead, each time the teacher activated the apparatus, the learner pretended to be in pain. The real object of Milgram's experiment was to see how far random participants would go in administering shocks of increasing intensity to strangers. The voltage meter was labeled descriptively as well as numerically. At the upper end of the scale, the labels read as follows: "Intense Shock," "Extreme Intensity Shock," "Danger: Severe Shock," and finally just "XXX." The impression that severe shocks were being administered was reinforced by the accomplice. At 150 V, he or she demanded to be released. As the voltage increased, his or her protests became more desperate. At 285 V, he or she screamed. After that, he or she made no sound at all.

Milgram (1974) expected most participants to refuse to administer shocks as soon as the learner demanded to be released from the experiment or very soon thereafter. Milgram planned to urge them to continue but expected the instructions to be disobeyed in most cases. In fact, participants were far more compliant than he expected. Typically, about 65% of all participants continued to administer the shocks all the way up to 450 V, well after the learner had ceased to respond. Almost all participants continued to administer the shocks up to 300 V. The experiment has been repeated all around the world with similar results.

What conclusions ought to be drawn from the Milgram (1974) experiment? According to the situationist critics of virtue ethics, what this experiment and many others devised by social psychologists show is that situation is more important than character in determining how people behave. Character traits, if there were any such things, would be dispositions manifested in a variety of situations. They would be relatively robust and relatively resistant to situational pressures. However, the Milgram experiment showed that the situation determines how the great majority of people will act. Thus, character, in the sense we ordinarily mean by this word, just doesn't exist. As Harman (1999) said

> It seems that ordinary attributions of character traits to people are often deeply misguided and it may even be the case that there is no such thing as character, no ordinary character traits of the sort people think there are, none of the usual moral virtues and vices. (p. 316)

Or, as another situationist critic put it, "to put it crudely, people typically lack character" (Doris, 1998, p. 506).

This follows, the situationist critics believe, because if there are such things as character traits of the sort both common sense and virtue ethics require, then people differ in which such traits they possess. However, if they differed in their possession of character traits, then they would act differently in different circumstances. Different people would respond in different ways when they are asked to administer electric shocks, or when they find a wallet, or when they are confronted with a stranger apparently in urgent need of assistance (to mention some of the experiments devised by social psychologists). Their character traits would manifest themselves regardless of situational differences. Yet they don't: It is the situation that determines how they behave. Hence, there are no such things as character traits in the form required by virtue ethics.

Now, the friends of character have not been slow to reply to these situationist criticisms. They have pointed out that what Harman (1999) and Doris (1998) have taken to be the settled findings of the science of social psychology are very much disputed within that science and that social psychology has itself produced evidence that reinforces the virtue-ethical notion of character.[2] They have argued that the situationist findings do not show that the virtues are nonexistent, merely that they are much harder to achieve than people would like to think. After all, there were some differences among people as to the extent to which they obeyed the instructions to administer the shocks (Athanassoulis, 2000). These critics have alleged that the results of the experiments actually support folk-psychological attributions of character traits, which are much finer grained than Harman (1999), in particular, allows for (Kupperman, 2001).

This debate is very much a live one, and philosophers would do well to be hesitant about drawing firm conclusions concerning its results. However, even as the evidence mounts that Harman's (1999) initial and relatively unnuanced rejection of the entire notion of character traits was too hasty, his conclusions remain unsettling for those people who reflect on the practice of journalism. Whether or not Harman was right in thinking that character traits do not exist in the form required by virtue ethics, the evidence he presented gives us reason to believe that reliance on character traits is not a good strategy for journalists.

Journalism and Moral Danger

Journalism is a morally dangerous profession. That is, journalism is one of a range of professions in which practitioners are regularly subjected to moral risks of one sort or another. In some professions, these risks involve the constant temptations of bribes or of abuses of power. In journalism, the moral dangers stem from the constant temptations to use deception. Deception is prima facie ethically objectionable; the more so in a profession whose entire raison d'être is the production of truth. Indeed, some media professionals have gone so far as to suggest that deception is always unacceptable. For instance, Ben Bradlee, a member of the Pulitzer Prize committee and a former editor of the *Washington Post*, explained the committee's refusal to award the prize to the *Chicago Sun-Times* for an exposé of municipal corruption that involved journalists operating a bar by arguing that journalists aim to uncover deception and therefore "simply cannot deceive" themselves (Luljak, 2000, p. 13). In fact, however, deception is frequently warranted. When it is the only way to reveal information that is in the public interest to know—when, in other words, it enables journalists to fulfil their role—its use is justified.

However, the fact that the use of deception is often legitimate makes it more dangerous, not less, for journalists. After all, the manner in which police officers ought to behave when they are offered a bribe is clear: They always ought to refuse it. Policing remains a morally dangerous profession because the temptation may sometimes be difficult to resist, but the correct action is always clear. For journalists, however, the dangers are increased precisely because the correct way to behave is often far from clear. Journalists frequently find themselves in situations in which they are unsure whether deception is warranted. They often cannot know in advance how important the information is they might uncover. They are frequently uncertain as to whether a particular activity falls within the domain of the public interest. In this kind of situation, the scope for self-deception abounds, and the journalist may well find himself or herself utilizing deceptive means on the slightest of pretexts.

*Character will be of little use in
guiding the behavior of
journalists ... situational factors
will determine whether or not
deception is used.*

Of course, it is precisely these kinds of dangers that those thinkers who emphasize the importance of the journalist's character have in mind. Their thought is that by ensuring that journalists have the virtue of honesty, society can best guarantee that they will not use deception lightly but will only utilize it when it is the best means of producing significant truth. I suggest, however, that character will be of little use in guiding the behavior of journalists because the situations in which the use of deception might be appropriate share significant features with the Milgram (1974) experiments. Accordingly, situational factors will determine whether or not deception is used.

What are the features of the Milgram (1974) experiment that made disobedience unlikely? Essentially, there were three, each of which has an analogue in the situation of the journalist considering the use of deceptive means. In the first place, participants in the Milgram experiment were reassured that the electric shocks they were apparently inflicting on the learner were harmless: painful but not dangerous. Of course, there was countervailing evidence to this assertion ranging from the screams and apparent lapse into unconsciousness of the learner to the labeling of the voltage meter ("Danger: Severe Shock" being not the highest but only the third highest shock the participant was asked to give). On the other hand—and this is the second feature of the experiment that made disobedience difficult—the reassurance came from an authority figure, a scientist in a white coat invested with all the prestige that science has in Western society. Finally, there was the feature that Harman (1999) himself pointed to, the fact that the shocks increased in intensity gradually so that the participants never had a clear sense that they were crossing an ethically significant line. As social psychologists like Ross and Nisbett argued, according to Harman (1999), "'The step-wise character of the shift from relatively unobjectionable behavior to complicity in a pointless, cruel, and dangerous ordeal,' make[s] it difficult to find a rationale to stop at one point rather than another" (p. 322). These three factors combine to intensify the situational pressures, almost guaranteeing that they will outweigh the resources of character, if indeed there are any such resources to be had.

What features of journalism mirror these situational pressures on the subjects of Milgram's (1974) experiment? First, there is the assurance that the shocks are not harmful. The analogue here is the assurance that the use of deception is not harmful. Of course, all journalists know that deception is potentially dangerous if, for instance, it were to lead to a decrease in trust on the part of the public. However, journalists can reassure themselves that these risks are worth taking. Deception can be an important means of reducing harms overall when it is used to uncover information that ought to be in the public domain but that is being hidden by unscrupulous politicians or businesspeople.

Second, and closely related to this first factor, there is the fact that reassurance concerning the use of deception comes from authority figures in the field. Journalists who hesitate to use hidden microphones or to adopt a false identity can take comfort in the example of such great investigative reporters as Woodward and Bernstein who used deception in uncovering the scandals of Watergate (Bok, 1978, p. 121).

Finally, and I suspect most important, there is the stepwise character of the use of deception. Journalists are very frequently encultured into its use in a gradual manner. An example from a study of a Midwest newsroom illustrates this process. The press had been banned from a certain area in a sporting stadium at the local university. The on-camera staff at the station could not violate this ban with any ease because their faces were too well-known. However, they had a student intern working for them at that point. She could enter that part of the stadium without attracting attention. There she conducted interviews using a hidden microphone (Luljak, 2000, p. 19).

Now, this particular use of deception is fairly innocuous. However, it is far from clear that any information could be obtained in this manner that would justify it. More important, however, it has the potential to set a young reporter on the road to a habitual use of deception. Although she was technically free to refuse to go along with the scheme, in practice, so doing was extremely difficult for her. She found herself on the verge of entering a very competitive market and needed good references from the station if she were to succeed. Moreover, she probably felt that she was not the person best placed to judge the merits of the case. Indeed, when Luljak (2000) asked her if she had any reservations about it, she told him that "having the news director behind me helped me know that I was right" (p. 19). At this point in her career, she felt unable to refuse the requests of her superiors and incompetent to judge the merits of the deception that she was asked to employ. At most, her responsibility for the scheme, which she did not initiate, was partial. She probably felt, rightly, that she was not crossing an ethically significant threshold because she was a minor player in a relatively insignificant ruse. However, by the time she is in a position to take full responsibility for such schemes, to initiate them, and carry them out herself, she will have been thoroughly socialized into a culture of casual deceit. She might go from this relatively innocuous case to more serious and totally unjustified invasions of privacy without ever having the sense that she has crossed an important line.

Conclusions

The situational pressures that characterize journalism, at least as it is structured today, are therefore likely to overwhelm the resources of character no matter how good our education, no matter how virtuous our students. If young reporters leave college and enter a workplace in which "deceptive reporting techniques [are] a standard form of journalistic behavior" (Luljak, 2000, p. 25), then reliance on the virtues is useless. Honest students will become deceptive reporters as easily as dishonest ones. So long as journalism is structured as it is presently, society can expect more cases like that of Janet Cooke.[3]

If this is the case, if virtue ethics is powerless, then how are regulators to limit the use of deception in journalism? How are they to ensure that it is used only when it ought to be, when it is the only means of uncovering information that is clearly in the public interest? The situationist critics of virtue ethics have constructive suggestions to make, as well as criticisms. John Doris (1998) is particularly useful here. Doris pointed out that if it is true that agents cannot rely on their characters to ensure that they behave ethically, they have other strategies that they can call into play. They can, for instance, refrain from entering into situations in which they will be put to the test (Doris, 1998, p. 516). Unfortunately, journalists cannot do this. As I have shown, journalism is unavoidably a morally dangerous profession in that deception will always remain a necessary tool for the investigative reporter. However, there are other ways of structuring the situation besides removing oneself from it altogether. Measures can be put in place to ensure that young reporters do not come under pressure to use deception. One way to do this would be to add a clause to codes of ethics barring journalists from such techniques during their 1st year of employment. This would ensure that they would not have to face ethical dilemmas when they are at their most vulnerable. Regulators might also consider means of structuring the rewards internal to journalism, from promotions to prizes and, most important, the admiration of one's peers so that those who use deceptive techniques are required to justify themselves before they are eligible for these rewards. Journalists cannot rely on character or virtue to inhibit deception, but regulators can structure the situation to reduce the pressure to employ it.

If these suggestions and the many others that creative professionals will no doubt invent were implemented, deception would become less commonplace, less routine in journalism. We would all live in a world in which there were fewer Janet Cookes. Indeed, if these reforms had been implemented earlier, fewer people would be exposed to the pressures to which Cooke herself succumbed.

This is not to say that good character is irrelevant to journalism. The advocates of virtue-centered approaches to ethical education are right to emphasize its importance. The point of these reflections is instead to stress the extent to which character formation is a process that requires a conducive environment, which is to say an environment shaped by regulations. If society is to produce virtuous journalists, journalists capable of resisting the pressures to deceive when it is not appropriate and when the regulations no longer guide them, it must focus at least as much on rules and structures as on character. The focus on character cannot be a substitute for the formulation of rules and guidelines for right action.

Notes

1. This is not the only end of journalism. As many people have pointed out, if legitimate journalism were limited to the functions mandated by the fourth estate conception, then a great many things that journalists actually do, from the reporting of sport to the covering of celebrity gossip, would be illegitimate. However, the fourth estate conception does provide the justification for behavior that would otherwise be ethically dubious. Use of entrapment techniques or of deception, for instance, is impermissible when there is no public interest as defined by the fourth estate conception in the information thereby revealed.
2. The best study to date of the extent to which social psychology actually supports the contentions of Harman (1999) and Doris (1998) is Steve Clarke's (2003) as yet unpublished "Courage Under Fire: Character Traits and the Fundamental Attribution Error."
3. The case of Janet Cooke is notorious among journalism professionals. In 1981, Cooke was awarded the Pulitzer Prize for her story about "Jimmy," an 8-year-old heroin addict, for the *Washington Post.* It later emerged that Jimmy was a fabrication. Cooke returned the prize and resigned in disgrace.

References

Athanassoulis, N. (2000). A response to Harman: Virtue ethics and character traits. *Proceedings of the Aristotelian Society, 100,* 215–221.

Belsey, A. (1998). Journalism and ethics: Can they co-exist? In M. Kieran (Ed.), *Media ethics*. London: Routledge.

Bok, S. (1978). *Lying: Moral choice in public and private life*. New York: Pantheon Books.

Borden, S. (1999). Character as a safeguard for journalists using case-based ethical reasoning. *International Journal of Applied Philosophy, 13*, 93–104.

Clarke, S. (2003). *Courage under fire: Character traits and the fundamental attribution error*. Unpublished manuscript.

Doris, J. (1998). Persons, situations, and virtue ethics. *Nous, 32*, 504–530.

Harman, G. (1999). Moral psychology meets social psychology: Virtue ethics and the fundamental attribution error. *Proceedings of the Aristotelian Society, 99*, 315–331.

Kieran, M. (Ed.). (1998). *Media ethics*. London: Routledge.

Klaidman, S., & Beauchamp, T. (1987). *The virtuous journalist*. New York: Oxford University Press.

Kupperman, J. (2001). The indispensability of character. *Philosophy, 76*.

Lambeth, E. (1990). Waiting for a new St. Benedict: Alasdair MacIntyre and the theory and practice of journalism. *Business and Professional Ethics Journal, 9*, 97–108.

Luljak, T. (2000). The routine nature of journalistic deception. In D. Pritchard (Ed.), *Holding the media accountable: Citizens ethics and the law* (pp. 11–26). Bloomington: Indiana University Press.

MacIntyre, A. (1985). *After virtue* (2nd ed.). London: Duckworth.

Milgram, S. (1974). *Obedience to authority: An experimental view*. London: Tavistock.

Journal of Mass Media Ethics, 19(2), 119–129

Stakeholders Versus Shareholders: Journalism, Business, and Ethics

Ian Richards
University of South Australia

❏ *Although the individual journalist is an essential unit of ethical agency, journalists are increasingly employees of large companies or corporations whose primary aim is to maximize returns to shareholders. Consequently, many, perhaps most, of the ethical dilemmas journalists face begin with the inherent conflict between the individual's role as a journalist and his or her employer's quest for profit. My underlying argument in this article is that this situation is not unique, that other fields are confronting similar dilemmas, and consequently, journalism may have much to learn from them. In the article I contend that business and journalism ethics, in particular, appear to have more in common than has generally been acknowledged and that the field of business ethics has yielded many concepts that appear to have relevance to journalism. In the article, I conclude that considering the insights offered by those who operate from the perspective of business ethics will facilitate analysis of the interface between individual journalists and the corporate forces that affect so many of them.*

Although the individual journalist is an essential unit of ethical agency, he or she doesn't operate in a vacuum. Most journalists are employees, and increasingly, employees of large companies or corporations, the primary aim of which is to maximize the return to shareholders. Although journalists are ultimately responsible as individuals, it is as individuals in a setting where their powers and duties are at least in part defined by their role in the corporate organization, and many, perhaps most, of the ethical dilemmas journalists face begin with the inherent conflict between the individual's role as a journalist and his or her employer's quest for profit. In its crudest form, this conflict manifests itself in a desperate quest for ratings and circulation on the part of particular media organizations, and in this form, the effects are often apparent to even the most casual observer because of the excessive zeal frequently displayed by reporters in the pursuit of news and current affairs with all that this entails for ethical deliberation and sensitivity.

In journalism generally, however, the pressures provoked by this conflict usually work in more subtle ways. Thus, editors and reporters may come under pressure from senior management to be more reader friendly to maximize ratings and circulation by, for example, taking steps to "increase advertising and subscription rates, to introduce cosmetic alterations of page design and makeup to give the impression of modernity, and to quietly reduce the amount of serious news" (Bagdikian, 1997, p. 83).

Such pressures are generally at their most intense following corporate takeovers. When such takeovers occur, it is not unusual for journalists to be faced with retrenchments and for there to be declining support for more expensive approaches to news gathering such as investigative reporting, greater use of material from sister outlets, a proliferation of lighter (and cheaper) stories about lifestyle, entertainment, celebrities, and so on, and a greater preparedness to use material provided through public and corporate relations (McChesney, 1999, p. 58).

The Context

Corporate takeovers generally have major ethical implications for journalism, not least because they challenge the underlying ethical justification for journalism. These implications, which have been traced elsewhere (Bagdikian, 1997; McChesney, 1999), are no less real in Australian journalism than elsewhere. As has been widely noted, the level of concentration of ownership of Australia's media is higher than in most other countries (Barr, 2000; Bowman, 1988; Chadwick, 1989, 1990, 1997; Cunningham, 1994; Edgar, 1979; Henningham, 1990, 1992; McQueen, 1977; Rosenbloom, 1978). As a result, many would argue, the corporate pressures on Australian journalists are correspondingly higher than in most other countries. As a result of this, most Australian journalists are employed in situations in which, as prominent journalist and former editor Michelle Grattan (1998) observed, "The bottom line has become hungrier and hungrier, and more and more the imperative by which performance, including the performance of editors, is judged" (p. 30). Symptomatic of this is the recent observation by a senior media executive in Sydney that

> In terms of content, there is no doubt that the consumer is more promiscuous than ever before, and that the only way to ensure that your relationship with him or her is more than a one night stand is to make the experience compelling. If all we do is report the news fairly and accurately, we haven't got a chance. (O'Reilly, 1998)

*Corporate takeovers generally
have major ethical implications
for journalism, not least because
they challenge the underlying
ethical justification for journalism.*

It is hardly surprising, then, that in recent years, Australian journalism has been marked by the rise of what *The Australian* newspaper's Paul Kelly (2001) has described as "the international show business trend" (p. 6). Indeed, a national study by the Australian Broadcasting Authority in 2001 found, in part, that the responses of news producers were dominated by the pressure of ratings and circulation, "reflecting the commercial imperative of modern news production," and that many news producers were "eager to give audiences what market research tells them they want" (Australian Broadcasting Authority, 2001, p. 7).

The ethical implications arising from this situation are considerable. They begin with what prominent Australian editor and journalist Max Walsh called "the perennial journalistic weakness of self-censorship ... which suggests that red-blooded, socially aware, concerned young men [sic] who join newspapers quickly learn to survive, but in order to survive they must toe the editorial line" (as cited in Major, 1976, p. 100). In Australia, "The dearth of alternative employers, the propensity to rationalise one's actions when preservation demands, and the excessive zeal of lieutenants are a combination potent enough to ensure plenty of self-censorship by journalists" (Chadwick, 1987, p. 7). This effect strongly encourages journalists to internalize the values of the news organization that employs them and to become conditioned into particular institutional conventions. The result can be a form of timidity, meaning that certain issues, views, or situations that rest uneasily with the corporate line will not be reported, exposed, or aired.

At the same time, many news outlets are encouraged by their corporate owners to give the greatest priority to finding and holding audiences that possess the qualities considered most desirable by advertisers in terms of levels of disposable income, education, occupation, age, and spending habits. Although this might be entirely justifiable in terms of business practice and the need to maximize profit, it is much more difficult to defend on ethical grounds because there are obvious losers from such an approach—the less well-off sections of society whose information needs and desires become understated or ignored altogether.

In this competitive corporate world, additional pressures on media outlets—and through them, individual journalists—arise because the demand for news appears to be waning in major markets around the world

(Light, 2000, p. 42). For the individual journalist, the net effect is that pressure to be first with the news and to get the story with the greatest audience impact is greater than ever. The ethical consequences of this situation can be considerable, for there is no shortage of evidence to demonstrate that "the fiercer the battle for circulation the greater the commercial pressures on editors to erode journalistic standards on matters of truth, accuracy and ethical acceptability" (Belsey & Chadwick, 1992, p. 45).

The corporatization of the newsroom and the corresponding extension of influence of corporate pressures on journalists raise other ethical questions. Media companies have often demanded special favors because of their power over public information, and there can also arise considerable pressure for using a corporation's media outlets to promote, or at least cover in a positive light, the operations of other sections within the corporation.

Underlying such issues is the fundamental question of how media organizations can provide information and analysis of the forces of corporatism when they are themselves an integral part of those forces. There appears to be an inherent conflict of interest involved, yet there is no acknowledgment of it, no reference to it, in any of the journalistic codes of ethics or practice. Indeed, most codes emphasize individual responsibility (McManus, 1997) and in so doing consistently fail to acknowledge the existence of this conflict. For example, many codes call on journalists to resist pressures from advertisers, thereby making the individual journalist responsible for withstanding such pressures when, generally, most of the power to stand up to advertisers lies with senior management.

In ethical terms, it is the audience that is the real loser from this situation. Most newspapers and broadcast news and current affairs programs claim to tell their readers, viewers, and listeners what is going on, and indeed, news and current affairs are one of the major external sources of information and opinion formation for most people. These people are ethically entitled to be able to rely on the accuracy and fairness of this information. Yet the forces of corporatism outlined previously are working to erode the validity of such expectations.

Australian media organizations have achieved a certain notoriety by calling for accountability and transparency from others while at the same time failing to be accountable and transparent themselves.

Further, these corporations are quite prepared to use the rhetoric of press freedom and the fourth estate as a bulwark against attempts at regulation, even when those attempts are grounded in the notion of accountability. Australian media organizations have achieved a certain notoriety by calling for accountability and transparency from others while at the same time failing to be accountable and transparent themselves. Through such behavior, the forces of corporatism are eroding journalism's claims, advanced under the umbrella of social responsibility theory, to service the political system by providing information, discussion, and debate on public affairs; enlighten the public so as to make it capable of self-government; and safeguard the rights of the individual by serving as a watchdog against government.

Discussion

At a theoretical level, one of the major weaknesses in many analyses of journalism ethics is the failure to accommodate the realities of corporatism. Although many acknowledge that there are problems arising from management and ownership pressures, much of the literature places the onus for ethical behavior squarely on the shoulders of the individual journalist and takes it no further. What appears to be needed is a coherent theoretical framework that facilitates incisive analysis of the interface between the practitioners in the field and the corporate forces that affect so many of them.

To develop such a theoretical approach, one could do worse than consider the offerings from other fields. One possibility is military ethics. After all, it could be argued that the central ethical dilemma of the individual journalist caught at the boundary of corporate responsibility is analogous to the individual soldier caught at the boundary of the evil military act. The Nuremburg Principles (Nuremberg Tribunal, 1950) of international law, intended to determine what constitutes a war crime, were developed to deal with precisely this dilemma, and they have proved to be as relevant in the aftermath of the unrest in Bosnia, Kosovo, and East Timor as at the trial of Lieutenant William Calley following the My Lai massacre and before him the Nazi hierarchy. These principles take their name from the tribunal that tried surviving senior Nazis after World War Two and include the principle that "the fact that a person acted pursuant to order of his Government or of a superior does not relieve him from responsibility under international law, provided a moral choice was in fact possible to him" (Principle IV; Nuremberg Tribunal, 1950).

It could be argued that similar principles apply to journalists whether employed in the corporate world of Rupert Murdoch, the BBC, or the Australian Broadcasting Corporation. However, there are many differences between the positions of journalist and soldier. The journalist's role and the justifications for this role are substantially different from the role and justifications for soldiering, even—perhaps especially—in times of war. Journalism's chains of command are less structured, and most journalists have far more autonomy in given ethical situations than the individual soldier.

A more appropriate field for investigation appears to be that of management in general and business ethics in particular. Admittedly, this is a somewhat disparate field—what one observer has described as "an uneasy hybrid of science, mathematics, psychology, social history and economics" (James, 1997, p. 48). Even the so-called father of management thinking, Peter Drucker, has stated that management is a liberal art rather than a science, and that "One problem is that it is afflicted by too many fads. I have been saying for many years that we are using the word 'guru' only because 'charlatan' is too long to fit into a headline" (James, 1997, p. 49). One of these fads is business ethics, a subject that has been taken increasingly seriously in recent years partly because of the widespread view that, in the words of an Australian business ethicist, "Business is the most powerful influence in most people's lives, therefore we need to understand business ethics" (Lagan, 2000).

This area has yielded many useful concepts, and some of these appear to have considerable relevance to journalism. One is the notion that at any given moment in most major corporations, one can find a vast array of vocabularies of motive and accounts to explain, excuse, or justify expedient action. This is also the case in journalism in which the much-vaunted public right to know is only the best known public justification.

Another useful concept when considering journalism ethics in a corporate setting is the notion of corporate culture, which has been defined as "the sum of all the values within the organisation ... arising from that organisation's history that ensures it has its own distinctive personality different to any other organization" (St James Ethics Centre, 1997, p. 1). Corporate culture produces what Jackall (1988) labeled "embeddedness": "People get embedded in their jobs, their positions in the company, and they have trouble seeing beyond the pressures they face. The result is a kind of blindness and an inability to see the larger view" (Jackall, 1988, p. 204). There is no shortage of examples of such blindness in the Australian media or in journalism generally.

A further concept from business and management that appears to be directly applicable to the news media is the notion of stakeholders, meaning individuals or groups of individuals affected by or able to affect the achievement of an organization's objectives (Boatright, 2000, p. 355). Stakeholders commonly include shareholders, management, employees, customers, suppliers, communities, and sometimes the environment. The notion of stakeholders provides an alternative model to the stockholder view of business, summarized in Milton Friedman's (1970) much-quoted statement that "the business of business is business" (p. 124).

The stockholder view is, briefly, that returns to shareholders have absolute priority over all other considerations with all that this implies for ethical standards. In contrast, the stakeholder view accepts that others have interests and rights of comparable weight. Although it is important to acknowledge the conceptual limits of stakeholder theory—there is, for example, a growing chorus that it is too blurred a concept to be of sufficient analytical use (Orts & Strudler, 2002, pp. 215–233)—the notion of stakeholders continues to be useful for identifying and organizing the multitude of obligations that corporations have to different groups (Boatright, 2000, p. 356).

Many if not most journalists are caught between conflicting allegiances to their proprietor, their newsroom managers, their colleagues, their sources, their audiences, and those whose activities they are reporting.

For this reason, the notion of stakeholders appears to be useful in journalism. In media organizations, the stakeholders include shareholders, management, employees (including journalists), readers, listeners and viewers, and also the wider community, although there is a considerable debate about what a community is or might be, and accordingly, it remains a somewhat confused and confusing notion. Although the stakeholder view has the advantage of extending ethical consideration to all of those affected by a corporation's internal and external activities, it also raises a fundamental dilemma: how to balance the conflicting interests of different stakeholders. This dilemma is not less acute in journalism than elsewhere because many if not most journalists are caught between conflicting allegiances to their proprietor, their newsroom managers, their colleagues, their sources, their audiences, and those whose activities they are reporting.

Most journalistic attempts to resolve this dilemma take into account the assumptions underlying social responsibility theory, itself echoed in the notion of corporate social responsibility. The latter involves corporations accepting responsibilities that go beyond the purely economic and legal responsibilities of business firms (Boatright, 2000, p. 340) and involves an acceptance of "a commitment to the public good that outweighs short-term individual self-interests" (Day, 1997, p. 34). Corporate social responsibility means, in effect, that corporate leaders take steps to bring corporate behavior up to a level "where it is congruent with the prevailing social norms, values, and expectations of performance" (Boatright, 2000, p. 340). The debates that have taken place over the validity of the notion of social responsibility in journalism are echoed in business. For example, there appears to be some conflict and indeed, confusion in the literature between descriptive and prescriptive interpretations of corporate social responsibility. The descriptive thesis suggests that, as a matter of fact, managers and corporations generally act in socially responsible ways, whereas the prescriptive thesis claims that regardless of the reality, they ought to act in socially responsible ways (Danley, 1998, p. 25).

Some sections of the Australian corporate world appear to have accepted that they have corporate social responsibilities, and indeed, there is a growing literature suggesting that good ethics is good for business (Abratt, Nel, & Higgs, 1992; Desai & Rittenburg, 1997; Enderle, 1997) and that corporations that pursue an ethical approach can improve the bottom line, win the approval of shareholders, and defuse the potentially negative effects of the growing movement toward ethical investment (Lagan, 2000). The converse of this is that poor ethics can be bad for business, and there is considerable evidence to support this view. In Australia, an increased focus on corporate ethics has developed against a background of disquiet over the behavior of public figures and institutions, from the corporate controversies of the 1980s to more recent scandals over, for example, the collapse of major insurance and dot-com companies. Yet, within the Australian media, the acknowledgment of corporate social responsibility and the acceptance of what it entails remain problematic. Indeed, sections of our media have been accused of being the last people to understand ethical obligations and the worst to deal with in terms of setting ethical standards (Lagan, 2000).

Many other questions that have been raised in business ethics echo those that have been raised in journalism. Thus, the complicated web of issues falling under the umbrella of conflict of interest and covering such matters as manager and employee relationships with clients and customers parallels the ethical issues that bedevil journalistic relations with sources. Those of us who are concerned with journalists ethics, for example, need to cultivate key informants to use as sources and at times come under pressure to present or not present their reports in certain ways to maintain a useful relationship with those informants. How they should manage those relationships—and how those relationships might be analyzed—may well be assisted by examining the ways in which business ethicists have advised managers how to deal with particular categories of client and customer.

Then there are the issues that have been raised around the notion of obligation. According to Provis (2002), managers encounter different sources of obligation and these different sources "pull us in different directions" (p. 2). Journalists and their editors also face many conflicting pressures, and journalism may well have something to learn from considering how others have analyzed their obligations and attempted to manage them in an ethical manner. Yet another focus of business ethics that has obvious relevance to journalism is the range of ethical dilemmas associated with the forces of corruption and bribery, especially—but not only—in non-Western countries. In management, this tends to focus on such matters as the awarding of contracts and doing business generally, but in the world of journalism, foreign correspondents, and their editors in particular, ask many similar questions.

> *Because issues of trust are as inextricably intertwined with contemporary journalism as they are with modern business, we appear to have something to learn from each other.*

Then there is the issue of trust, which has emerged as a key issue in business and is surely just as central to the world of journalism. After all, how can journalists have credibility with audiences without their trust? Indeed, why should anyone trust the news media in the first place? One of the contradictions of our era is the way in which a widespread lack of trust of traditional institutions—including business and the media—seems to go hand in hand with a remarkable level of naïve trust in fringe cults, religions, get-rich-quick schemes, and so on. Journalism is at the center of this contradiction, and journalists might well benefit from considering how others have approached it. For example, business ethicists appear to have some useful insights into such issues as the conditions that need to be met before one party will or should trust another, whether trust is static or dynamic, and whether trust can be repaired once it has been broken or betrayed (Flores & Solomon, 1997; Koehn, 1997). The underlying point is that because issues of trust are as inextricably intertwined with contemporary journalism as they are with modern business, we appear to have something to learn from each other.

Finally, it is worth remembering that the underlying force that drives business ethics is the same basic question that underlies journalism ethics: Why be ethical? This is not always an easy question to answer, and we have all met practitioners and senior managers who have told us that ethics is a luxury they can't afford. Surely those of us who are trying to encourage such individuals in the direction of ethical behavior should be prepared to consider the approaches developed by others in the face of similar responses, regardless of whether they operate in a business or journalistic environment. Indeed, given that journalism is increasingly operating in a context that straddles both environments, the case for doing so appears to have become overwhelming.

References

Abratt, R., Nel, D., & Higgs, N. (1992). An examination of the ethical beliefs of managers using selected scenarios in a cross-cultural environment. *Journal of Business Ethics, 11*, 29–35.

Australian Broadcasting Authority. (2001, May). *Sources of news and current affairs: A research report in two stages conducted by Bond University for the Australian Broadcasting Authority.* Sydney, New South Wales, Australia: Author.

Bagdikian, B. (1997). *The media monopoly* (5th ed.). Boston: Beacon.

Barr, T. (2000). *Newmedia.com.au: The changing face of Australia's media and communications.* Sydney, New South Wales, Australia: Allen and Unwin.

Belsey, A., & Chadwick, R. (Eds.). (1992). *Ethical issues in journalism and the media.* London: Routledge.

Boatright, J. (2000). *Ethics and the conduct of business.* Upper Saddle River, NJ: Prentice Hall.

Bowman, D. (1988). *The captive press.* Ringwood, Victoria, Australia: Penguin.

Chadwick, P. (1987, December). A charter for independence. *Australian Society, 6* (12), 5–7.

Chadwick, P. (1989). *Media mates.* Melbourne, Victoria, Australia: Macmillan.

Chadwick, P. (1990). The ownership disaster: How journalism failed. In J. Henningham (Ed.), *Issues in Australian journalism* (pp. 221–232). Melbourne, Victoria, Australia: Longman Cheshire.

Chadwick, P. (1997, Winter). Too few have had too much for too long. *The Walkley Magazine,* 8–9.

Cunningham, S. (1994). Diversity: Rhetoric and reality. In J. Schultz (Ed.), *Not just another business* (pp. 115–130). Leichhardt, New South Wales, Australia: Pluto Press.

Danley, J. (1998). Beyond managerialism: After the death of the corporate statesperson. *Business Ethics Quarterly, The Ruffin Series, 1*, 21–30.

Day, L. (1997). *Ethics in media communications: Cases and controversies.* New York: Wadsworth.

Desai, A., & Rittenburg, T. (1997). Global ethics: An integrative framework for MNEs. *Journal of Business Ethics, 16*, 791–800.

Edgar, P. (1979). *The politics of the press.* Melbourne, Victoria, Australia: Sun Books.

Enderle, G. (1997). Worldwide survey of business ethics in the 1990s. *Journal of Business Ethics, 16*, 1475–1483.

Flores, F., & Solomon, R. (1997). Rethinking trust. *Business and Professional Ethics Journal, 16*(1–3), 47–76.

Friedman, M. (1970, September 13). Social responsibility of business is to increase its profits. *New York Times Magazine,* pp. 122–126.

Grattan, M. (1998, July 29–30). The selling of journalism. *The Walkley Magazine, 7*, 30.

Henningham, J. (Ed.). (1990). Is journalism a profession? In J. Henningham (Ed.), *Issues in Australian Journalism* (pp. 129–162). Melbourne, Victoria, Australia: Longman Cheshire.

Henningham, J. (1992). *Journalism's threat to freedom of the press.* Melbourne, Victoria, Australia: The Book Printer.

Jackall, R. (1988). *Moral mazes.* New York: Oxford University Press.

James, D. (1997, September 15). Peter Drucker, the man who changed the world. *Business Review Weekly*, p. 48. Retrieved March 20, 2003, from LexisNexis academic universe database.

Kelly, P. (2001, June 13). *Keynote address.* Paper presented at the Media Traditions Conference, University of Central Queensland, Rockhampton, Queensland, Australia.

Koehn, D. (1997). Trust and business: Barriers and bridges. *Business and Professional Ethics Journal, 16*(1–3), 7–28.

Lagan, A. (2000, August). *Corporations and ethics.* Paper presented at the Meeting of Postgraduate Journalism Students, University of South Australia, Adelaide, Australia.

Light, D. (2000, June 27). The last post. *The Bulletin, 118,* 41–45.

Major, G. (Ed.). (1976). Mass media in Australia. *Proceedings of the 41st summer school, Australian Institute of Political Science.* Sydney, New South Wales, Australia: Hodder and Stoughton.

McChesney, R. (1999). *Rich media, poor democracy.* Urbana: University of Illinois Press.

McManus, J. (1997). Who's responsible for journalism? *Journal of Mass Media Ehtics, 12,* 5–17.

McQueen, H. (1977). *Australia's media monopolies.* Melbourne, Victoria, Australia: Widescope.

Nuremberg Tribunal. (1950) *Principles of international law recognized in the charter of the Nüremberg Tribunal and in the judgement of the Tribunal.* University of Minnesota Human Rights Library. Retrieved January 20, 2004, from http://www1.umn.edu/humanrts/instree.1950a.htm

O'Reilly, C. (1998, September 3). *The Media report* [Radio interview]. Sydney, Australia: ABC Radio National.

Orts, E., & Strudler, A. (2002). The ethical and environmental limits of stakeholder theory. *Business Ethics Quarterly 12,* 215–233.

Provis, C. (2002, October). *Organisational politics, personal relationships and dirty hands.* Paper presented at IIPE Conference, Reconstructing The Public Interest in a Globalising World: Business, the Professions and the Public Sector, Brisbane, Queensland, Australia.

Rosenbloom, H. (1978). *Politics and the media.* Melbourne, Victoria, Australia: Scribe.

St James Ethics Centre. (1997, Autumn). The ethics of merging. *Living Ethics, 27.* Retrieved September 3, 2002, from http://www.ethics.org.au/things_to_read/living_ethics_our_newsletter/index.htm.

Journal of Mass Media Ethics, 19(2), 130–137
Copyright © 2004, Lawrence Erlbaum Associates, Inc.

Empowerment as a Universal Ethic in Global Journalism

Tom Brislin
School of Journalism
University of Hawaii at Manoa

❑ *Globalization has churned up in its wake a reevaluation of standards in numerous enterprises, including journalism. The search for a universal journalism ethic, however, has often ended with the attempt to import traditional and underlying Western "free press" values, such as objectivity and an adversarial platform, forged in Enlightenment philosophy. This belief of the universal portability of Western values is reflected in the mixed results of several professional initiatives in the early and mid-1990s designed to both install and instill a First Amendment-based free press system in the newly independent former states of the Soviet Union. Scholars admonish that modernization through globalization is not Westernization and warn of the futility of attempting to fit indigenous values into a procrustean bed of Western economic or political design. Multiple models of citizen–press–government relationships grow legitimately out of indigenous value systems and are endurable within the forces of globalization. This does not mean the search for a universal journalism ethic should be abandoned to the morass of cultural relativism, but rather that a new starting point should be found and new focal points enumerated. Globalization has produced several major paradigm shifts in world societies, not the least of which is increasing degrees of autonomy of both the individual and the citizenry to encourage a wider participation in both the governing and economic process. This suggests that a new focal point of journalism ethics should be empowerment—the degree to which a society's journalism is designed to empower the citizenry for its own betterment rather than the degree to which it creates a passive audience of consumerism. In this study, I advance an ethic of empowerment that can both reflect the changes of globalization and respect indigenous value systems. I also argue that a principal structural measurement of this global ethic should be the degree of autonomy the journalist enjoys, within legal, cultural, and professional limits.*

Globalization has churned up in its wake a reevaluation of standards in numerous enterprises, not the least of which is journalism. Global-centered research has focused attention on both national systems of journalism and on the intercultural nexus where differing systems meet (Brislin, 1997, 2003; Cohen-Almagor, 2002; Jirik, 2001; Luther, 2002; Zhang, 2001). Because perspectives are most often limited by personal and professional experiences, these studies most often involve the concepts, standards, and practices of Western journalism pitted against some other culturally distinct system.

Western-style journalism has been acclaimed a model for global journalism but for the most part by Western-style journalists and scholars. Certainly the technology that has driven advances in journalism in North America and Western Europe has been adopted and adapted across the world. Even the smallest islands of the Pacific are capable of desktop-based publishing for both traditional print and electronic Web-based distribution.

With that production technology is an assumed template of a standardized form, content, and approach to the production of news and the production of meaning in journalism. The dominance of a few North American and Western European media corporations in providing international coverage also assumes a positive role model in newspaper, news magazine, and broadcast journalism that local outlets will follow in the thought that consistency carries the cachet of credibility.

Globalization certainly dictates certain consistencies and standards among cooperating nations to enhance trade and other commercial—and political—interests. The European Union (EU), forged in the democracies of Western Europe, insists on passing marks on a report card of standards as the price of admission for Eastern European states eager to join. These standards encompass not only economic reforms but human rights reforms as well, including guarantees of a free, if not unfettered, press. For some Eastern European dissidents, joining the EU is not so much emerging into the sunlight after years of darkness behind the Cold War Iron Curtain but rather simply shifting into the shadows of influence of one system from those of another. Although modernization is embraced, Westernization is not.

*Modernization through
globalization is not
Westernization.*

Similar discontents at increasing attempts to hegemonize Western standards and practices in the cloak of globalization are heard in the Pacific, East Asia, Africa, and certainly in West Asia and the Mideast. Samuel Huntington (1996), in *The Clash of Civilizations: Remaking of World Order,* and others have admonished that modernization through globalization is not Westernization and have warned of the futility of attempting to fit indigenous values into a procrustean bed of Western economic or political design.

The traditional journalism-state paradigms themselves have come under review. Jennifer Ostini and Anthony Y. H. Fung (2002) found the traditional four theories of the press wanting in a post Cold-War age and proposed a new model of national media systems. Ostini and Fung noted that the Soviet Communist and social responsibility theories were really subsets or outgrowths of a two-world view: libertarian and authoritarian, or the West versus the "Rest."

Ostini and Fung (2002) proposed a paradigm matrix that attempts to accommodate not only the continuum of state-controlled and private news media (a democratic and authoritarian axis) but also the individual journalistic values that drive the newsrooms that comprise the system (a conservative and liberal axis). The paradigm matrix, Ostini and Fung argued, can encompass such similar and diverse systems as the United States (democratic and liberal) and Japan (democratic/conservative), and the People's Republic of China (authoritarian and conservative) with its new Special Autonomous Region of Hong Kong (authoritarian and liberal).

Ostini and Fung's (2002) reconsideration of a state-journalism to a state-journalism-journalists paradigm is an important reframing for the discussion of whether a standard and consistent global journalism ethic can be found, as it

- Recognizes there is legitimate variation within the Western/democratic systems, just as there is considerable variations within the Rest, or non-Western systems, that cannot be so easily pigeonholed into Cold War worldview categories.
- Recognizes there are legitimate and considerable variations within media systems themselves between the industry values of owners, whether state or private, and the professional values of the journalists.

Variations in journalistic practices, standards, and values within the traditionally defined Western-democratic nations and similar variations within news organizations themselves between the profit-centered owners and managers and the professionalism-centered journalists make a one-size-fits-all code both unlikely and unworkable. Yet the search for a universal journalism ethic has often ended with the attempt to import traditional and underlying Western free-press values, such as objectivity and an adversarial platform forged in Enlightenment philosophy.

This belief of the universal portability of Western values is reflected in the mixed results of several professional initiatives in the early and mid-1990s that were designed to both install and instill a First-Amendment-based free-press system in the newly independent former states of the Soviet Union.

Some ... are questioning
whether the ... journalistic
imperatives of truth telling,
independence, and minimizing
harm ... continue to be workable
in a journalism industry whose
source of guidance is not Main
Street but Wall Street.

Some scholars and practitioners are questioning whether the traditional (albeit newly coined) journalistic imperatives of truth telling, independence, and minimizing harm—based on the ethical triumvirate of virtue, duty, and consequences—continue to be workable in a journalism industry whose source of guidance is not Main Street but Wall Street and whose profit-centered organizational structures are models for responses to globalization rather than community building (Carter, 2002). Likewise, there is discussion in the academic community on whether the study and application of abstract ethical theories to documented or hypothetical cases have true generalizability to newsroom operations, as the context for the classroom is an idealized journalism rarely, if ever, found in the actual industry context.

Taking the view that ethics is a subset of professionalism, as professionalism is composed of several sets of standards based on both intrinsic and extrinsic values, it would be worthwhile to conduct comparative studies of professionalism as a key step in trying to divine a global or universal ethic. Professionalism must exist in the real-life context of contemporary journalism, not in an abstract universe where situations can be deconstructed and rebuilt with a solid mortar of principle. Meaningful standards and practices are those that professionalism can support. U.S. media scholars often talk about ethical values being trumped by competing values. Obviously, ethical values must be in the same suit as professionalism's for them to have winning, if not honors, value.

Recent comparative studies (Cooper, Christians, Plude, & White, 1989; Gunaratne, 2000, 2001; Merrill, 1991) have demonstrated that even within the state systems generally perceived to be most restrictive and oppressive, there is a sense of professionalism among its journalist practitioners whether or not their medium acts as an agent of the state. Just as the professionalism of Western journalists provides them a degree of independence from the bottom-line, full-profit structure of the media in which they operate, the professionalism of, for instance, Chinese journalists offers them a degree of independence from even the purely unidirectional propaganda structure of the media in which some operate (Jernow, 1993; Jirik, 2001; Zhang, 2001).

Autonomy is a critical defining difference between a propagandist and a journalist.

Autonomy is a critical defining difference between a propagandist and a journalist. Although truth telling is certainly regarded as the prime imperative of Western journalists and even heralded as a universal imperative by international journalist organizations, it is autonomy that in direct proportion makes the reporting and disclosure of truths possible. Of course, scholars, jurists, and even U.S. Presidents argue differing standards of truth, from social construction and postmodernism to DNA evidence to the meaning of "is" and what constitutes a sexual relationship.

Journalists talk about reporting the "best version of the truth," "reasonable truth," and even "practical truth." Chinese journalists, in an earlier, more repressive era, told me, "We can tell our readers the frequencies for *Voice of America* and other international news programs, but should we— knowing it will put them in harm's way, as it will ourselves?" (J. Yu, personal communication, September 1984). More recently, journalists from China have echoed that sentiment. "We can tell our readers how to find the mirror sites for suppressed world wide web home pages for CNN or MSNBC, but we would be telling them what they already know, and only get ourselves in trouble" (F. Qiu, personal communication, September 2001). Although conventional wisdom paints such regimes as China as opponents of the truth in the drive to promote other nationalistic values, John Watson (2002) showed that the U.S. Supreme Court devalued truth to promote other values, such as civil rights and even a free press, in its landmark *Times v. Sullivan* ruling.

Although truth is an admirable imperative, it is also a very spongy one—difficult to measure and subject to multiple claims and self-justifying interpretations. Autonomy, on the other hand, is equally admirable and somewhat easier to measure. One observable trend of globalization and its major paradigm shifts in world societies is increasing degrees of autonomy of both the individual and the citizenry to encourage a wider participation in both the governing and economic process.

An argument can reasonably be made that the autonomy of journalists is reflective of (although not necessarily proportional to) the autonomy of the citizenry in any given state. Autonomy empowers journalists to practice their professionalism, which in turn offers the potential to empower the citizenry. Professionalism itself is, of course, empowering, as it allows the journalism to hold to values that are not subsumed by the prevailing system—whether rampant capitalism or state-directed authoritarianism.

> *The autonomy of journalists is reflective of (although not necessarily proportional to) the autonomy of the citizenry in any given state.*

Journalists, within their professional roles, make scores of micro-decisions that whittle the core of a truth, that select the frame through, and angle from, which it will be seen, the amount of it that will be revealed, the tone in which it will be presented, and how it will be summarized, punctuated, edited, packaged, and delivered. Journalists deal in truth as a raw material in the production of meaning through storytelling. The degree to which they put truth through these journalistic processes for the purposes of empowering their constituents is a measurable ethic. Even in the most open of democratic societies, news media can inform with truthful dispatches (think supermarket tabloids, a version of reasonable truth) without empowering.

The U.S. "civic" or "public journalism," vested in (some would say swamped by) the values of communitarianism, would propel journalism along a path of empowerment through its advocacy for community building, perhaps at the expense of more traditional values or practices of dispassion, objectivity, and a framework of adversarial relationships. Many Western European, Japanese, Taiwanese, and Korean news organizations are comfortable with an advocacy model, in effect "wearing their politics on their sleeves," achieving balance in the aggregate rather than within each organization.

These press systems are notable for treating their constituents as active citizens, directing them in ways to participate in their respective polities. The mainstream U.S. press, bound in what some would call a cult of objectivity, is often criticized for emphasizing problems without solutions, treating politics as a spectator sport rather than a participant sport, and for treating its constituents as consumers. (This is not to say that consumers can not be empowered to be activist in their pursuit of a reformed and fair capitalist system. However, the current models of globalization seem to have no place for its discontents nor provisions for providing them a voice. Although specific policy criticism is welcomed in U.S. journalism, there is little room for systemic criticism, particularly following September 11, 2001.)

The question and challenge remain: Is empowerment a reasonable measuring stick and standard for "the Restern world"—the multitude of non-Western systems that are fellow travelers on the superhighway of globalization? Ostini and Fung's (2002) re-realized state-press-practitioner paradigm of Democratic and Authoritarian and Conservative and Liberal would allow empowerment as an intersecting vector. Its strength would be driven not only by the degree of autonomy offered to both journalists and citizenry but also—and more important—by the conscious application of the journalists' professionalism for the benefit of the citizenry.

Future studies of comparative press systems, practices, standards, and values should include a focus on the degree of autonomy the journalist enjoys within legal, cultural, and professional limits and how that autonomy is translated into an ethic of empowerment that both reflects the changes of globalization and respects indigenous value systems.

References

Brislin, T. (1997, February). *An update on journalism ethics in Asia: Values and practice as context for meaning in Japan, China and Korea.* Paper presented to the Association for Practical and Professional Ethics, Washington, DC.

Brislin, T. (2003). Anti-semitic articles & books not uncommon in Japan. *Japan Media Review,* USC Annenberg School of Communication. Retrieved September 26, 2003, from http://www.ojr.org/japan/media/1064022502.php

Carter, H., III. (2002, April). *Celebrating the past, focusing on the future.* Paper presented at the James K. Batten Awards and Symposium for Excellence in Civic Journalism, Pew Center for Civic Journalism, University of North Carolina at Chapel Hill.

Cohen-Almagor, R. (2002). Responsibility and ethics in the Canadian media: Some basic concerns. *Journal of Mass Media Ethics 17,* 35–52.

Cooper, T., Christians, C., Plude, F., & White, R. (1989). *Communication ethics & global change.* New York: Longman.

Gunaratne, S. (2000). *Handbook of the media in Asia.* Thousand Oaks, CA: Sage.

Gunaratne, S. (2001, August). *Freedom of the press: A world system perspective.* Paper presented to the Association for Education in Journalism and Mass Communication, Washington, DC.

Huntington, S. (1996). *The clash of civilizations: Remaking of world order.* New York: Touchstone.

Jernow, A. (1993). *Don't force us to lie: The struggle of Chinese journalists in the reform era.* New York: Committee to Protect Journalists.

Jirik, J. (2001, August). *What is the state of the emperor's new clothes? An investigation into the Chinese news media as the mouthpiece of the party and government.* Paper presented to the Association for Education in Journalism and Mass Communication, Washington, DC.

Luther, C. (2002). National identities, structure, and press images of nations: The case of Japan and the United States. *Mass Communication and Society, 5,* 25–40.

Merrill, J. (1991). *Global journalism: Survey of international communication* (2nd ed.). New York: Longman.

Ostini, J., & Fung, A. Y. H. (2002). Beyond the four theories of the press: A new model of national media systems. *Mass Communication and Society, 5,* 25–40.

Watson, J. (2002). *Times v. Sullivan:* Landmark or land mine on the road to ethical journalism? *Journal of Mass Media Ethics, 17,* 3–19.

Zhang, Y. (2001, August). *Four effects in the professionalization process: A study of the Chinese reform era.* Paper presented at the Association for Education in Journalism and Mass Communication, Washington, DC.

Journal of Mass Media Ethics, *19*(2), 138–148

Cases and Commentaries

The *Journal of Mass Media Ethics* publishes case studies in which scholars and media professionals outline how they would address a particular ethical problem. Some cases are hypothetical, but most are from actual experience in newsrooms, corporations, and other agencies. We invite readers to call our attention to current cases and issues. (There is a special need for good cases in advertising and public relations.) We also invite suggestions of names of both professionals and academicians who might write commentaries.

In this issue, we are departing somewhat from our usual style of case presentation. Sharon Schnall, a freelance journalist in Ohio, wrote the essay we present here. She invites the reader to reflect on a variety of issues and circumstances. Except for using fictitious names and titles, her essay is an entirely true presentation of her actual experience.

Louis W. Hodges, Editor
Knight Professor of Ethics in Journalism, Emeritus
Washington and Lee University
Lexington, VA 24450
(540) 458–8785

A Lesson in Self-Defense Challenges One Editor

My teary-eyed son approached me, his coach close by his side. An impromptu playground game among four boys got out of control, the coach said. In the end, one boy had encouraged two other boys to send soccer balls in my son's direction. A black and white soccer ball hit his head and wounded his pride.

[I sort through what happened and advise, "Sometimes you have to walk away from bad behavior; other times you have to get help."

"But, there will be times," I tell my son, "when you just have to stand your ground and fight back."]

The next day, I followed that advice as I confronted an editor about ethics versus writing ability.

As a freelance writer, I work with editors of all sorts: city editors, managing editors, and editors-in-chief. They suggest additional questions to pose to my subject, a better lead, or different sequencing. Copy editors verify the facts both big and small and clarify attribution. "Did your subject say this?"—they verify. "Which subject said that?"—they clarify. All guide my writing toward an improved final product.

With appreciation for the editorial process, I waited for feedback from "Sarah," my editor, concerning a feature she asked me to write. I am not a newcomer to Sarah's publication, having worked first for Naomi, the editor-in-chief, and Deborah, the business development editor. Still, it is my first opportunity to work for Sarah, a health editor, and I anticipate a break-in phase.

The message on my answering machine was harsh; Sarah said she has problems with my work. Were there gaps in the story? I wondered. Would she request more information?

I called Sarah. "You have all the facts but I don't like your organization. … It lacks schmaltz and joviality," she said.

My news correspondent's experience does not lend itself to the free-flowing style she prefers. She wants less factual attribution and more descriptive text. Her editorial approach is different. With 2 weeks remaining before deadline, she will not have me incorporate her suggestions. Rather, she rewrote the feature. "Look it over and make sure there aren't any inaccuracies," she said.

I have written for numerous publications, each a little different from the next. Now, I will learn to develop the freer style Sarah desires. I read and reread her e-mailed version. Unfortunately, I do not discover schmaltz or joviality. Rather, Sarah has copied text from an article, about the same subject, which recently appeared in another publication.

Indeed, the words she copied and paraphrased made for an interesting read. Also, she added a fabricated quote, attributed to the subject and his wife, the latter of whom was never interviewed.

[I tell my son, "When you cannot stop the behavior you have choices: Getting help is one choice."]

The next day I phoned Naomi, the editor-in-chief. "I have a problem with using text from another publication in this feature," I said. "What do you mean text from another publication?" Naomi replied, her surprise and discomfort evident. "Sarah copied text from another article." I unloaded everything.

Naomi made several declarations about unacceptable practices. I faxed and e-mailed documents for her review. An hour later, she delivered the verdict: "You are both partially to blame," she concluded.

[The friendly playground game is changing. The players have re-grouped. The balls are no longer being thrown back and forth. All are directed at me, hard and fast, and it hurts.]

"Sarah has admitted to using the text from the other article and creating the husband and wife's quote." Again, Naomi said this is unacceptable. However, Sarah told Naomi, and Naomi concurred, that my writing approach triggered this editorial intervention.

Was this the same editor-in-chief who recently wrote a righteous editorial following the revelations about *New York Times* writer Jayson Blair's plagiarism and falsification of information? In her editorial about upholding journalistic standards, Naomi wrote that one falsification by a reporter was one too many, and termination of employment is the only course of action; there can be no trust.

I told Naomi how impressed I was with that essay, reciting the title and date of publication in case she has forgotten her strong stand. She laughed nervously. Perhaps that editorial was the fashionable piece to write, not necessarily a reflection of her true convictions; it is easy to criticize others but not so simple when faced with a similar situation.

[Remember, sometimes you have to hold your ground and fight back.]

I listened as she critiqued my writing style. "Your feature reads like a medical textbook. You were supposed to write about this man's humanitarian efforts," she said. "It's just rat-a-tat-tat, fact after fact."

Why hadn't this criticism been raised when my other features appeared in this same publication? Had my writing deteriorated overnight? I waited for the criticism to end. Eventually, she quieted down. It was my turn to comment: "Whenever I write for a new editor, I expect to develop a style to fit that editor's preferences. But you are confusing writing skill and plagiarism. I cannot share the blame."

[If you fight back, especially with the bully, you can demonstrate your strength.]

I unwittingly activated every defensive nerve in Naomi's body. Still, I understood what was happening. At our constructive best, we thank persons for bringing problems requiring corrective action to our attention. At our defensive worst, we lay the blame elsewhere, which is what Naomi did.

She said this is the first time Sarah has ever plagiarized or falsified information. She hesitated and qualified: This is the first time it has ever come to light. Sarah will remain in Naomi's employ.

I stayed calm and did not return the personal attacks. Nor was it appropriate to discuss with Naomi how she prefers to deal with Sarah's actions. "This is a personnel matter for you to handle," I said. I asked that my byline be removed from Sarah's version, and I told her that I expected payment in full for this work.

Naomi agreed to my terms. She said she is making an exception. I have no desire to keep the money. If paid, I will donate it.

[The balls are no longer being lobbed. I say goodbye and gladly restore the phone to the cradle. I am done with the playground bully.]

Will the editor-in-chief wrestle with any conflicting emotions? Are Naomi and Sarah friends? Perhaps Sarah is an employee whom Naomi has mentored over the years. Will Naomi closely review Sarah's work or hide behind denial, forgetting about this cavalier plagiarism and falsification?

My own demons gnawed at me. Hadn't I seen the staff's different journalistic bent in previous encounters? Did my desire for publishing credentials blind me? Was my writing substandard?

[The next day, my son returns to the playground. Before the playing begins, he tells his friends how he got hurt. The playing resumes and so does the ball throwing.

"Stop," he tells the instigator, "You can't throw balls at people." The throwing stops and he states his position. The boys and my son run off to play. I am surprised by the outcome and proud of his straightforward approach.

One boy, the instigator, fidgets with the soccer ball as the others regroup. No doubt he has not changed, but for now his desire for playground mayhem is deterred.]

Nor have the editors changed—a little shaken possibly but positioned to move on.

And, what about the writer? Within a day, I was back to work, disappointed but also moving forward, already thinking about the next story idea.

By Sharon Schnall
Chagrin Falls, Ohio

Commentary 1
The Mother Should Have Mimicked Her Son

The mother gave good advice to her son, but she didn't apply it to herself. "Sometimes you have to walk away" is advice the writer should follow. She should walk briskly away from Naomi's publication and never do business with her again.

Only with that heroic act will Naomi realize that she is only kidding herself with her phony, ineffective handling of this outrageous situation. Strong action is necessary to force Naomi to come to grips with her own hypocrisy. Naomi has an employee who plagiarized and fabricated—two of journalism's biggest sins. Rather than facing that serious journalistic breach with courage and directness, she brushed it under the rug and alleged that the writer's bad writing caused the journalistic sin.

Sarah's weakness and total disregard for journalistic standards caused the breach, not the original writing, no matter how bad it was. By her action, Sarah, as an editor, has told the entire magazine staff "there are no standards here." By supporting her, Naomi has endorsed that lack of standards in 96-point type.

Journalists need to decide now, in 2004, whether we are going to be guided by the standards of truth and verification as endorsed by Bill Kovach and Tom Rosenstiel (2001) in *Elements of Journalism*, or we are going to succumb to the temptations of the easy fix. Kovach and Rosenstiel presented five clear, easy commandments to live by:

1. Never add anything.
2. Never deceive the audience.
3. Be as transparent and open about your motives and methods as possible.
4. Rely on your own individual reporting.
5. Exercise humility.

However, the headlines tell us plagiarism and fabrication are spreading, and worse, some readers and journalism students are telling us they are not sure what the big fuss is about.

Let's be clear about this once and for all; these are compelling reasons journalists should do their own work and not plagiarize.

- It is honorable.
- It assures accuracy. You are not counting on anybody else to get the facts right.
- It builds confidence and credibility in your work that you cannot guarantee if it comes from somewhere else.

- Using someone else's work is theft, pure and simple. You are stealing another person's effort and presenting it as your own.
- It's impersonation. You are pretending to be somebody else. You are pretending to be a better reporter or a better writer than you really are. You are pretending to be more ambitious and resourceful that you really are. You are an impostor!

Plagiarism, fabrication, and misrepresenting where we are when we write the story are unacceptable, and all editors and publishers—including Naomi—need to do more than wring their hands with editorials. They need to act firmly and decisively when they see the kind of plagiarism and fabrication Naomi saw in this case. However, Naomi took a powder and sacrificed her standards to protect her editor, and she abandoned her ethical responsibilities as a manager when she did.

Naomi's choice to blame the writer for Sarah's sin violated a concept I have been calling "ethical stewardship." It is the concept of instilling in an organization the values and ethics required to make the right moral choices to overcome all the problems that organization faces. My notion of ethical stewardship would force us to consider as ethical issues many things that we now view as routine corporate imperatives. Allocations of resources, training, rewards, job design, and yes, reasonable, achievable deadlines are all issues the ethical steward must consider.

If we examined all those issues in the context of rights, responsibilities, and duties, our workplaces would be far healthier. If Naomi had examined the writer's writing style problems in this way, she would have come to a very different conclusion. If the writer has not written in the style the publication wants, we must ask, were those expectations clearly explained? Did the company train its writers in this new style? Shouldn't the writer have been apprised of the specific problems with specific suggestions before Sarah rewrote the piece?

Well-designed jobs with firm expectations are essential. As simple as it sounds, employees must know what is expected of them and many do not. It is amazing how many companies tacitly expect people to pick up processes, guidelines, and expectations out of the air. Formal training and sharing of expectations is essential and it is the ethical thing to do.

If Sarah and Naomi had examined their responsibilities to the writer and thought about the writer's rights, they almost certainly would have taken different actions.

Also, it is just as important to consider the writer's duties. If the writer is simply failing to respond to training and clearly explained expectations, Sarah has an ethical obligation to be firm. Confronting the employee is the only ethically correct thing to do. "Being nice" is not ethical if it means we let the underperforming employee skate on her responsibilities.

That confrontation must be compassionate, but it also must be firm and clear. It is crucial that you make sure the behavior is the issue and not the goodness of the human being, and it is vital that you don't let the person off the hook. She must take responsibility.

Sarah and Naomi seriously failed the writer and the profession. Our mother/writer did not effectively mimic her son. She did not tell Naomi and Sarah to stop their behavior. To do that, she must walk.

References

Kovach, B., & Rosenstiel, T. (2001). *Elements of journalism*. New York: Crown Publishers.

By Tim McGuire
Syndicated Columnist and Author

Commentary 2
Preventing Plagiarism: What Does a Journalist Need To Do?

Sharon Schnall points out something that happens at least once in every journalist's professional life: that moment when an editor's role changes from the normal journalistic process into plagiarism. In broadcasting, it happens too, but perhaps less often than in print. It's just harder to invent the quote when you are counting on the audio or video interview to substantiate the editorial direction of the report. Still, it can happen.

A reporter will "set up" the clip giving listeners or viewers an expectation of what they are about to hear: ("But President Bush didn't agree with the Democratic leadership. TAKE AUDIO OF PRESIDENT BUSH ..."). The audio that follows should confirm the scripted "lead-in," as it is called.

However, what if the audio is from another context? Has the reporter inappropriately inserted the audio to make his or her point? Digital editing makes that process more easily and expertly done. We are fortunate that today's broadcast reporter is less likely to get away with it. In the age of Internet information and a proliferation of sources, nothing can be hidden.

A case in point: Senator Robert Torricelli of New Jersey misspoke himself in an interview. He said he would appeal a ruling to the Supreme Court. He meant the New Jersey Court of Appeals, which functions as the state's supreme court. Listeners would understand it to mean the United States Supreme Court—which would place the story in a whole other legal, political, and journalistic context.

Rather than add that information to a news report on National Public Radio (NPR), the editor inserted the word "state" from another part of the interview. It was Torricelli's voice. He just hadn't spoken it in the audio clip. Listeners quickly informed NPR that there was something wrong with the interview. A few pointed out they had watched Torricelli on C–SPAN and knew that he had misspoken. NPR management quickly aired a correction, and the editor was reprimanded.

The Torricelli case qualifies as bad reporting, but it is not plagiarism as such. In this case, I think the (milder) punishment fit the misdemeanor.

Plagiarism is worse. It occurs when there is a distortion to change the meaning and editorial content of a story or to cover up the inadequacies of the reporting.

It is deliberately and consciously dishonest, which is a fireable offense in most news organizations.

In the rush to deadline, mistakes are made. Not all of them are deliberate or deserve the most extreme punishment, but a clear explanation of practices and policies in a news organization goes a long way to keeping mistakes—both great and small, deliberate and accidental—from getting on the radio.

Some examples and practices from broadcasting are the following:

• Using audio or video from another source and not telling the listener that it comes from the BBC or CBS. The listener might be left with the assumption that the reporter actually got the interview himself or herself.

• Use of "foreign" audio for wartime reports. One bomb sounds much like another, but the sound of explosions must come from the event being reported, not from old or "stock" footage.

• Sound effects must never be used. A radio reporter filed a story on the failing fish industry. The editor rejected the story as "dull" and said it needed some audio from the harbor. The reporter was close to deadline and knew he could not get down to the docks and back in time. So he cheated and found some audio of seagulls in the library. A listener who happened to be an eminent ornithologist said he was sure he heard a Great Lakes seagull in a story from Newfoundland—more than 2,000 miles to the east.

• Overwriting. Although writing for the ear should always be "visual" and allow the listener to imagine the scene, the writing should not be melodramatic. A reporter must not allow his or her emotions to color the story by presuming an emotional intensity that is not there. It is suggested that overwritten and overwrought reporters try writing a script without adverbs or adjectives as a corrective.

• "Sign offs." This is the audio signature in radio. The reporter identifies him or herself, the news organization, and the dateline or place where he or she has done the report. For some reason, the phrasing of a sign off evokes huge internal debates at NPR. Some stories will have only "Jane Doe, NPR News" as a sign off. This indicates that the reporter was not on the scene but has assembled the story from wire copy. Other reporters will have interviews from a variety of locations—Mosul, Baghdad, and Istanbul, to quote one recent report from Ivan Watson on NPR. Watson filed the report to NPR from Istanbul, but he had interviews he had gathered some days before from inside Iraq. Rather than imply that he was recently at all those places, he signed off "Ivan Watson, NPR News." This was to avoid the issue raised in the recent *New York Times* imbroglio when a reporter used a dateline but was never physically in that place.

• TV news used to superimpose the word "File" whenever stock footage was used in a news report. It seems to be rarely used these days, possibly because fewer television reporters are doing the same level of original reporting. I have no solid information on this, but my guess is that reliance on stock footage has increased.

Because broadcasting is both a linear and an impressionistic medium, listeners or viewers can't revisit the story that was just aired to see if the first impression was correct. Broadcast organizations have to make sure that the bond of trust they have with their listeners is not breached either in custom or observance.

Schnall has the same two options as her readers: to stay because she believes (as do her readers) that the editorial process is trustworthy or to leave and look for a more rewarding journalistic experience.

By Jeffrey A. Dvorkin
National Public Radio
Washington, DC

Commentary 3
Naomi Handled the Freelancer's Whistle Blowing Inappropriately

Experienced journalists come to appreciate that their stories are not entirely theirs. Aside from the legal issues in this case and others, there is the reality that journalism is a team effort. What you turn in to your immediate supervisor and what actually gets published or broadcast probably will not be the same. The consolation is that the editing process usually makes your story better. The reason is that reporters and editors usually share certain values: accuracy, clarity, impact, and so on.

That being said, there is a sense in which a news story is the unique property of its author. The specific words used, the specific quotations included, and the specific sources consulted all reflect the writer's abilities, expertise, and labor. The best editors recognize this aspect of authorship and try to improve stories without unnecessarily diluting the reporter's voice—or worse, having the writer appear to be speaking in an entirely different tongue.

The freelance writer in this case is confronted with an editing process that turns these assumptions upside down. Sarah's disrespect for others' work is clear when she wholesale rewrites the freelancer's story rather than giving her an opportunity to try again. Sarah effectively deprives the freelancer of meaningful control over her own work and tries to impose authorship, in a way, by attaching the freelancer's byline to copy she can barely recognize. We in journalism have been focusing on the reverse problem lately—depriving freelancers, stringers, and interns of bylines that news organizations rightfully owed them. However, the reverse also has moral implications.

The ethical stakes are that much higher when we add plagiarism and fabrication to the mix. Fabrication violates journalism's basic promise to strive for truthfulness and is thus an obvious moral offense. What's the big deal about plagiarism? Plagiarism often gets categorized as a form of stealing, and rightly so. However, it is not just words or phrasing that get stolen; along with these, the original author is unjustly deprived of the benefits accompanying authorship. American journalists work in a society that recognizes and rewards property ownership, individual autonomy, and original expression. When peers fail to respect each other's ideas, discoveries, and words, the associated goods flow unjustly to the thief rather than to the rightful beneficiary. It is not just the original author who suffers injustice; the employing news organization also becomes a victim of theft because it is unfairly deprived of the benefits associated with financing, publishing, and copyrighting the author's work.

Clearly, the American conception of plagiarism relies on a Western understanding of property rights and individuality. However, given that this is the context in which American journalists work, it is legitimate to attribute moral significance to the well-established expectation that you may not use what is mine without my permission. It's not just the work itself that is my property—it's the credit for creating that work, acknowledgment that it is I who made it.

However, there is more to plagiarism than stealing. There is deception also. Plagiarists mislead others about their role in creating the work and about who truly deserves credit for it. This has the effect of misleading members of the public about the source of the ideas and information they are receiving. They are thus deprived of a crucial resource for evaluating the story's reliability. In this way, plagiarists break faith not only with their peers but also with the public.

These are some of the reasons why journalists have cultivated respect for quotation marks and bylines. Notice that the freelance writer in this case insists, above all, that her name no longer be associated with the controversial feature story. In a significant sense, it is no longer hers. She also does not wish to be associated with disrespecting another writer's work or misleading readers.

However, in this case, nothing has actually been published. Has anyone been robbed or deceived at this point? Not technically, it seems. However, if editor-in-chief Naomi forges ahead with Sarah's version and does nothing but remove the freelancer's byline, the ethical liabilities discussed earlier remain for the original author, the author's employer, and the readers of Naomi's newspaper. Others suffer, too. The newspaper, even if the plagiarism is never publicized, loses integrity and may be more likely to commit plagiarism in the future. If discovered, the paper also may pay a price in credibility, morale, and other costs. The staff gets smeared too and may feel betrayed, much like the *New York Times* staffers post-Blair.

Further, Sarah's actions warrant sanctions. The fact that she would so casually commit both plagiarism and fabrication just for the sake of snappy copy raises the specter of prior incidents that simply have not come to light yet. This may not only require disciplinary action but perhaps also a correction of the record.

Even if there have not been prior incidents, what does this one say about Sarah's allegiance to public commitments the newspaper has made to readers and staff? Is Sarah prone to cutting corners, or is this an aberration? Can she be trusted in the future? There are many contextual factors Naomi would have to consider before deciding how to deal with Sarah, including any special relationship they may share. Maybe the zero-tolerance policy Naomi endorsed in her editorial was unwise. Nevertheless, it clearly is inappropriate simply to do nothing where Sarah is concerned.

Finally, Naomi has handled the freelancer's whistle blowing inappropriately. Sure, defensiveness is a common human reaction to criticism, but punishing the freelancer for reporting wrongdoing is foolish and unfair. The freelancer is doing Naomi and the paper a favor. Do Naomi and Sarah think no one else will notice the plagiarized portions of the article? As evidence from the recent Jayson Blair scandal at *The New York Times* suggests, perhaps the sources of the story would not have reported the made-up interview, but that is not a given. Sarah's actions subject the paper to justified criticism and attacks on its credibility. Maybe Naomi can't pull herself together enough to say "thank you," but at least she should not blame the freelancer for Sarah's plagiarism and fabrication.

By Sandra L. Borden
Associate Professor of Communication
Co-Director, Center for the Study of Ethics in Society
Western Michigan University

Journal of Mass Media Ethics, *19*(2), 149–155
Copyright © 2004, Lawrence Erlbaum Associates, Inc.

Book Reviews

The Book Review Editor has moved! She is now the Poynter–Jamison Chair of Media Ethics and Press Policy at the University of South Florida St. Petersburg.

Deni Elliott
Department of Journalism and Media Studies
The University of South Florida St. Petersburg
St. Petersburg, FL 33701
E-mail: elliott@stpt.usf.edu

Ethics is Essential in Teaching Effects Research
A Review by Lee Bollinger

Sparks, G. (2002). *Media effects research.* Belmont, CA: Wadsworth. 221 pp., $53.95 (Hbk).

A scan of the table of contents of this research text surprisingly includes a chapter about Marshall McLuhan and his "ascientific" ideas. This I found very appealing. Also, I was enthusiastic as I read the opening paragraph of the first chapter in which Sparks discusses the Columbine shootings and points out that there was a consistent theme over and over again that "the mass media must share a significant part of the blame for this incident" (p. 1). I hoped, then, that I would see more statements about media responsibility (and ethics). However, I observed rather quickly that missing from this carefully planned how-to-do-research book were statements to the effect that ethics should be the underlining of all research projects. I am sure that Sparks assumes it will be, and there is mention of the "ethics of research" when protecting children as subjects. In another later section, Sparks discusses media effects studies and how researchers "must be concerned about the ethics of subjecting subjects to potentially harmful media messages" (p. 180).

Certainly, as Sparks points out, any study involving humans and media messages (visual, auditory, or written) requires caution. However, and this is really my concern with this text, practicing ethical research inquiry in any form is not part of either a chapter of its own or a threading throughout the chapters.[1] What comes to mind is research that involves content analyses (coding media political coverage or an organization's press releases or electronic media messages) and miscounting or miscoding or falsifying data. In another chapter, Sparks encourages students to think about future research that focuses on the activities displaced by heavy television viewing (p. 64). Perhaps, he suggests, symptoms such as marriage decline, social network reduction, and even a decline in civility could be studied with regard to viewing habits (p. 69). However, a follow-up statement, not made, might have been regarding the possibility of studies about the ethical values (not quite the same as civility) of a group of people and correlations with amount of television viewing, for example.

In the chapter about effects of media violence, here again the topic of ethics could have been inserted. Sparks introduces the chapter with an example of the "copycat phenomenon"—people imitating exact behaviors they see depicted in the media (p. 72)—and explains the concern to protect children and what they see on television. He presents questions to the reader, among which is, Would copycat criminals eventually commit their crimes even if a TV program or movie never inspired them to act? (Here missing is a suggestion for research about the accountability of networks and producers of violent programs.) Although there may be gaps in here about ethics, there are no gaps about the subject of drawing hasty conclusions. One statement Sparks makes throughout the text, which is so important, is a cautionary one to readers about making inferences. Sparks writes, "No matter how strong the tendency to think otherwise, it is important to recognize that content does not equal effect" (p. 75).

Further, Sparks's ideas for research topics are noteworthy. For example, in a short discussion of the desensitization hypothesis, Sparks concludes that future research should include studies about why people like violent entertainment, for example, why violence is so attractive to some people. However, missing again is any mention of the ethical values of these viewers as well as television and movie producers, much less networks that air violent shows. Also missing from this same discussion is any mention of the ongoing argument about whether media values reflect society's values.

Still, the chapter topics are noteworthy. Two chapters include discussion of the effects of sexual content in the media and the phenomenon of frightening media. Again, Sparks cites important studies in search of answers about the effects of visual and verbal depictions of sexuality and many shows on the paranormal, which are often the most frightening to children and adults (p. 111). Again, not mentioned is the subject of media responsibility. It is not as if there were no studies about media and accountability and media as mere messengers.[2] In my opinion, student researchers should be made aware of such questions about ethics on the part of filmmakers or networks and conduct studies that search for an answer to the question, Is it ever appropriate to blame the messenger?

One cannot, however, cite this text for lack of style. For example, in a chapter about sexual content in the media, Sparks interjects discussion with a personal touch: "Sometimes, a case of strange bedfellows (pun intended again) can be found in debates about sexual content" (p. 91); and "A few years ago, I had the chance to talk with one media researcher who had published some results that showed negative effects of being exposed to pornography" (p. 92).

Further, what I found myself thinking while reading the discussion about agenda setting and its offshoot, framing theory, was how Sparks was (stylistically) framing the discussion. He offers a vivid example of how media might frame news in a community after a major snow storm and in doing so gives readers an example of how a news medium might concentrate on, for example, the community's inadequate snow removal system. In other words, Sparks frames for us, as an example, an inept arm of public works that is believable because it is possible. In Sparks's explanation of the work of Elisabeth Noelle-Neumann, he explains the spiral of silence theory concisely and on the student's level: "(The theory) is based on the idea that most of us don't feel very comfortable speaking out about our views if we perceive that we are in the minority" (p. 157). (Teachers can easily relate this to moments of hesitation students often exhibit about speaking out in classes.) The author makes it clear in this chapter that the media can affect what we think about and what we think in general, and I would propose to students, How ethical is media intrusiveness?

While on the subject of how media affect us, the author writes about Dale Earnhardt's fatal crash and how news video footage was "dramatic and highly emotional" and then writes, "Thanks to new video technology, viewers were able to see what the crash looked like from Earnhardt's perspective from inside his car" (p. 161). Although the point being made by the author is that people remember news based on emotional arousal, I would have preferred the statement had it started with "Because of new video technology ..." instead of "thanks to new video technology."

The next two chapters include the effects of media stereotypes and the impact of new media technologies. Sparks, thankfully, includes a discussion of the impact of video games and a discussion of "killology." What is important here are two points. One is the systematic way that Sparks explains that there have been few (p. 30) studies completed on video game effects and two, how people pointed to violent video games as the cause of the Columbine shootings because both shooters had been fond of playing the video game *Doom*. He cautions the student readers about making hasty conclusions and suggests that we think instead about Eric Harris, one of the shooters, as being in the "high-risk category" for potential criminal behavior (p. 197). Not mentioned here again are the ethical issues involved in accessing information on the super highway, the Internet, or the responsibility of video game producers, much less media accountability in the coverage of Columbine.[3]

The last chapter, devoted to Marshall McLuhan, is anything but irresponsible; it is irresistible. It catches the reader off guard and turns out to be my favorite chapter. The author's intent here is to explain to students that just because an analysis cannot be tested and proven to be right, it may not ever be proven to be wrong either (p. 201). What better way to show students in a research class that there are always ideas that cannot be proven false because they are beyond scientific scrutiny. What better way than to provide examples by way of McLuhanisms—the global village, medium as message and as massage, hot and cool media, and technological determinism. This was a nice way to end the text and provide a last minute alternative to the scientific approaches to research. Yet, Sparks makes it clear that just as McLuhan cannot be ignored, neither can he be given scientific applause. However, he is definitely worth thinking about—and remembering (p. 215).

To sum it all up, I would have preferred a little more mention of ethics, especially in sections about violent messages, subliminal seduction, and emotional responsive programs that the media (television and film) continue to churn out. I would have preferred mention about ethical dilemmas faced by businesses that sponsor arousal and subliminal seductive advertising (even if the latter supposedly is viewed by the Federal Communications Commission as unorthodox). I would have preferred a how-to research text that also mentions, in some fashion, responsibility and ethical decision making. I like the text. I will use it in a senior-level research class. I will offer a caveat as well.

Notes

1. See Paula M. Poindexter and Maxwell E. McCombs (2000), *Research in Mass Communication* (Boston: Bedford/St. Martin's), in which there is mention throughout the text of ethics in research (e.g., surveys, analysis, procedures, and training coders in ethical standards).
2. Two reviews in the *Journal of Mass Media Ethics*, Volume 16, Number 1, 2001, cite recent texts: "On Not Blaming the Messenger: Media and Civic Virtue," A review by Stephen Ward; and "Media Accountability: A French Perspective," A review by Deni Elliott.
3. In the discussion of a text called *Media Ethics* (2002) in which Columbine is used as a case study, Lee Wilkins presents this question for students: What is the news media's overall responsibility in combating societal problems such as the violence at Columbine?" (p. 43; Patterson, Philip, & Lee Wilkins (2002), *Media ethics*, 4th ed., Boston: McGraw-Hill).

❏ *Lee Bollinger is an assistant professor in journalism and mass communication at Coastal Carolina University.*

Understanding Journalists' Ethical Decisions
A Book Review by Kimberly Wilmot Voss

Wicker, T. (2001). *On the record: An insider's guide to journalism.* Boston: Bedford/St. Martin's. 164 pp., $31.95 (Pbk).

In a time when Jayson Blair and Stephen Glass are household names, the ethical practices of journalists are under a microscope. Although a vast majority of journalists don't plagiarize the work of others or fabricate sources, ethical calls are woven into the creation of stories each day. Tom Wicker takes on those day-to-day decisions in *On the Record: An Insider's Guide to Journalism.* The book lives up to its "insider's guide" claim by offering an analysis of the decision-making processes used by journalists. Wicker, a former associate editor of *The New York Times,* watched as large and small ethical decisions were made during his 25 years at the newspaper.

Wicker writes that his intent is to describe what journalists do as well as why and under what limitations. He does not deny the mistakes made under the guise of competition or profit. In one of his criticisms, he takes the journalistic practice of "being first" to task. In a time when publication can be immediate, he questions whether being first is as much of an issue as it once was. Instead, he writes that getting it first should not be the priority over getting it right. He takes on the slippery concepts of truth and objectivity in the lives of journalists. His premise is that journalism is a business without rules. Rather, the field is guided by abstractions that are fluid. What is news? How important is it? Why isn't press freedom balanced with press responsibility? To make sense of the decision-making process, Wicker applies broad principles to actual cases in chapters ranging from journalistic choices to bedroom issues to the trustworthiness of eyewitnesses to the impact of competition.

Wicker's strongest points are in his chapter about facts. He challenges the concept of objectivity as a way for journalists to avoid making an ethical call. By simply including an equal number of facts, reporters can use objectivity to "avoid criticism from both sides." This reliance on just reporting facts means that there is no context given to a story; rather, the reporter lets the facts "speak for themselves." Wicker argues that journalists have an ethical responsibility to provide a foundation for those facts. He applies the theory to the journalistic coverage of Senator Joseph McCarthy's crusade to out alleged Communists. The reporters covering the senator's accusations failed to investigate the issues and to speak to experts who could have challenged McCarthy's claims. "Too often, Objective Journalism simply propagated his words and just as dutifully reported—also without significant comment or context—the protests and counter-charges of the politicians, academics and others with nerves and knowledge enough to challenge Tailgunner Joe" (p. 82).

Wicker addresses the cynicism of the media's function by allowing that journalists make mistakes, but they do not intentionally mislead the public by printing an untruth. The trickier question that Wicker nicely investigates is the exact nature of truth in a story. Although journalists may not be intentionally writing "untruths," it doesn't mean that the media's credibility is growing. He writes that distrust of the media has led some people to wonder if the media have too much freedom. Wicker cites national surveys as well as his experiences in the classroom. His defense is little—falling back on the mantra of many journalists. "There are two realistic options before the American people: (a) government control and probable government manipulation of news reporting or (b) the sometimes chaotic, sometimes pernicious, often beneficial diversity of a free press" (p. 154).

The strength of the book is Wicker's application of ethical decision making to regular newsroom practices. With a few exceptions, Wicker's examples are those that journalists in any metropolitan newsroom will encounter such as whom to quote and which quotes to use. So often, ethical examples are based on extremes rather than the typical situations that a majority of journalists will encounter. In another practical application, Wicker argues that journalists have an ethical obligation to look beyond stories fed to them by official sources. He details the many stories that are overlooked when journalists rely too much on the status quo. He urges journalists to cover schools by doing more than going to school board meetings and to cover hospitals by looking beyond malpractice lawsuits. His biggest criticism is of the lack of court coverage.

A downfall of the book is the lack of philosophical framework for the decisions that are made. This book would be an excellent additional reader for a media ethics class that already has an philosophically based textbook. It would also work well as an addition to a philosophy class to provide nonmedia students with an understanding of how the industry functions. It could help those students understand that ethical decisions are not made in a sterile environment but rather in complex newsrooms clouded by deadlines, competition, and past practices. As Wicker writes, "Reporters are not automatrons nor computer chips nor mere news 'tickers'" (p. 88).

❏ *Kimberly Wilmot Voss is an assistant professor in the Department of Mass Communication at Southern Illinois University, Edwardsville.*

Books Received

Bracci, S. L., & Christians, C. G. (2002). *Moral engagement in public life*. New York: Peter Lang. 296 pp., $32.95 (Pbk).

Bimber, B. (2003). *Information and American, technology in the evolution of political power*. 268 pp., $22.99 (Pbk).

Bird, S. E. (2003). *The audience in everyday life*. Chicago: Taylor & Francis/Routledge. 211 pp., $23.95 (Pbk).

Bryant, J., Roskos-Ewoldsen, D., & Cantor, J. (2003). *Communication and emotion*. Mahwah, NJ: Lawrence Erlbaum Associates. pp., $89.95 (Hbk).

Ecarma, R. E. (2003). *Beyond ideology*. Lanham, MD: University Press of America. 129 pp., $28.99 (Pbk).

Hargreaves, I. (2003). *Journalism, truth or dare*. New York: Oxford University Press. pp., $19.95 (Hbk).

Horten, G. (2002). *Radio goes to war: The cultural politics of propaganda during World War II*. Berkeley: University of California Press. 218 pp., $45.00 (Hbk).

Jackall, R., & Hirota, J. M. (2000). *Image makers, advertising, public relations and the ethos of advocacy*. Chicago: The University of Chicago Press. 333 pp., $18.00 (Pbk).

Liebovich, L. W. (2003). *Richard Nixon, Watergate, and the press*. Westport, CT: Greenwood. 143 pp., $45.00 (Hbk).

Maxwell, R. (2003). *Herbert Schiller*. Lanham, MD: Rowman & Littlefield. 176 pp., $22.95 (Pbk).

Olasky, M. (2003). *Standing for Christ in a modern Babylon*. Wheaton, Illinois: Crossway Books. 160 pp., $12.00 (Pbk).

Tarbell, I. M. (2003). *All in the day's work*. Champaign: University of Illinois Press. 412 pp., $21.95 (Pbk).

Thomas, D. (2003). *Hacker culture*. Minneapolis: University of Minnesota Press. 288 pp., $19.95 (Pbk).

Verney, K. (2003). *African Americans and US popular culture*. New York: Routledge. 130 pp., $17.95 (Pbk).

Wilson, C. C., II, Gutierrez, F., & Chao, L. M. (2003). *Racism, sexism, and the media*. Thousand Oaks, CA: Sage. 327 pp., $39.95 (Pbk).

Wolf, M., & Perron, B. (2003). *The Video game theory reader*. Chicago: Taylor & Francis/Routledge. 343 pp., $22.95 (Pbk).

*For Product Safety Concerns and Information please contact
our EU representative GPSR@taylorandfrancis.com Taylor & Francis
Verlag GmbH, Kaufingerstraße 24, 80331 München, Germany*

T - #0160 - 270225 - C0 - 229/152/5 - PB - 9780805895346 - Gloss Lamination